DOUGHNUTS

90 Simple and Delicious Recipes to Make at Home

2nd Edition

LARA FERRONI

SASQUATCH BOOKS
SEATTLE

CONTENTS

INTRODUCTION

When I was growing up, doughnuts were the exception, not the rule. They were reserved for one very special time: the road trip. Each summer our family of four would pile into our ridiculously small car and head out across the country to visit an aunt or cousin or grandparent. Trips going west meant little boxes of sugared cereal eaten at a roadside Holiday Inn. But trips northward meant the best thing imaginable to my eight-year-old self: Dunkin' Donuts.

My brother always ordered the chocolate dipped. I would stand on my tiptoes and carefully examine each flavor, imagining how the pastry would feel and taste as I took my first bite. Despite careful deliberation, I always decided between the same two flavors: the Chocolate Kreme Filled and the Dunkin' Donut. The Dunkin' Donut was about as simple as it gets: an old-fashioned cake doughnut with a hint of spice ingeniously shaped with a handle for dipping into a fresh cup of joe. I never actually dunked my doughnut, but I liked the little handle anyway. The Chocolate Kreme Filled was a fluffy raised doughnut filled with almost fluffier milk-chocolate frosting and coated with powdered sugar.

While I'll always love those doughnuts, my tastes have also expanded. My husband, who hails from Hamilton, Ontario (the birthplace of Canada's famous doughnut shop Tim Hortons), turned me on to the ethereal Honey Cruller. When I lived in Seattle, it was hard to avoid the temptations of Top Pot (Raspberry Glazed Chocolate Old Fashioned!) and Mighty-O (French Toast!), and all too easy to make a quick drive north of the city to Frost (Bourbon Caramel Pecan!). When we moved to Portland, we indulged in Voodoo Doughnut's wonderfully crazy creations, like the Dirt, and Blue Star's Crème Brûlée doughnut with a Cointreau injection. Now that we are living in DC, it's all about Sugar Shack's eclectic flavor of the moment, like the seasonal Harry Potter–themed

Butterbeer doughnut (insider tip: Sugar Shack churns out new batches and flavors all day, so ask for whatever just came out), and Astro Doughnuts and Fried Chicken, where you can get a fried chicken sandwich with honey and hot sauce on an Old Bay doughnut. We even traveled to San Francisco to gorge on Dynamo Donut's eclectic varieties and, of course, sampled the offerings at New York's Doughnut Plant, and Peter Pan Donut and Pastry Shop.

Being surrounded by all those glorious pastries made me wonder if maybe, just maybe, I could make doughnuts at home. The notion of a fresh, warm doughnut pushed me past my initial deep-frying anxiety. How glad I am that it did! Making doughnuts is far simpler than I could have imagined, and my fear of hot oil was quickly banished. Before long I was dreaming up flavors for my own sinfully satisfying doughnuts, and was lucky enough to share the best of those recipes in the first edition of this book.

While a few years have passed, here I am, still fascinated with developing new techniques and flavors for homemade doughnuts, and still delighted to share them with you. In this second edition, you'll find new doughs, glazes, toppings, and fillings to mix and match. So go ahead, treat yourself. You'll be happy you did . . . and so will those around you!

DOUGHNUT BASICS

Before you get started with your first batch of dough, I encourage you to read through this section for an overview of doughnut making and general tips and tricks on ingredients and tools.

HOW THIS BOOK IS ORGANIZED

The first section of recipes is all about the basics of doughnut making. In it, you'll find recipes for raised and cake doughs, including chocolate doughs, doughs that can be baked instead of fried, and doughs for vegan and gluten-free diets. You'll find many well-known specialty doughs—like old-fashioned sour cream, ricotta, apple cider, and French cruller—as well as some that are less familiar, like *picarones* from Peru and *malasadas* from Portugal. You'll also find recipes for basic glazes that work with these doughs—mix and match to your heart's content.

For something a little more special, turn to the Flavors chapter (page 80), where you'll find even more interesting combinations, from Apple Pie to Crème Brûlée. Each of these recipes refers back to a dough recipe type. Pick the dough that works best for you (traditional, baked, vegan, or gluten-free), then follow the recipe as directed.

If you're planning ahead, it is worth noting that unfilled, unglazed dough-nuts can be frozen once they are cooled. To reheat, microwave for eight to ten seconds.

A note for those cooking vegan and gluten-free doughnuts: Not all of the variations on the basic recipes include vegan or gluten-free instructions, but most should be easily convertible by using readily available substitutions. Gluten-free doughnuts can be a bit harder to fill than their wheat-based counterparts because by their very nature they are denser. To make things a bit easier, use a chopstick to hollow out the middle of the doughnut before using the piping tip.

INGREDIENTS

For best results, all your ingredients (including milk, eggs, yogurt, sour cream, and butter) should be at room temperature when they are used.

Flour

Choose your flour based on which type of doughnut you are making. Hard, high-protein flours, such as bread flour, work best for yeast-raised doughnuts. However, if your doughnuts are a bit too tough or heavy, try a blend of bread and unbleached all-purpose flours. Unbleached all-purpose flour is best for cake doughnuts, but if your doughnuts fall flat when removed from the fryer, next time mix in a little bread flour.

Different flour brands have different protein contents and densities, both of which can dramatically affect the consistency of the dough. Even the humidity of the day can change how much flour fills up a measuring cup. It is best to use weight measurements if you can, but if you need to use cup measurements, use the spoon-and-swipe method on freshly sifted flour. You may still need to adjust the amount of flour in the recipe to achieve the perfect consistency based on your flour brand. I typically use either King Arthur flours or a locally grown and milled flour that measures between 120 and 140 grams per cup.

If you can't eat wheat, I think you'll be quite pleased with the gluten-free raised and cake doughnuts in this book. Doughnuts require a very lightweight gluten-free baking mix that doesn't have a strong flavor. My friend and author Shauna James Ahern helped me develop a terrific gluten-free flour mix for doughnuts for the first edition of this book.

Since that time, many gluten-free flour blends have come on the market, and I've learned even more about gluten-free baking. While I still recommend the original blend for the cake doughnuts, I prefer a blend based on Gluten Free on a Shoestring's Better Than Cup4Cup blend for yeast doughnuts, which are fairly finicky when it comes to the ratio of protein to starch needed to give a fluffy dough. Without the gluten (or without using things with "modified" in their name), you'll never quite get the same airiness as a wheat-based doughnut, but these doughnuts have a gorgeous, almost creamy crumb I think you'll love.

Gluten-Free Baking Mix for Cake Doughnuts

MAKES ENOUGH FOR A STANDARD CAKE DOUGHNUT RECIPE

1 cup (175 grams) potato starch
½ cup (60 grams) tapioca starch
½ cup (60 grams) sweet rice flour
¼ cup (100 grams) potato or sweet sorghum flour

• In a small bowl, combine all the ingredients. Store in an airtight container until ready to use.

Gluten-Free Baking Mix for Yeast Doughnuts

MAKES ENOUGH FOR A STANDARD YEAST DOUGHNUT RECIPE

⅓ cup (54 grams) tapioca starch
⅓ cup (54 grams) nonfat dry milk
¼ cup (108 grams) white rice flour
3 tablespoons (66 grams) brown rice flour
3 tablespoons (66 grams) cornstarch
2 tablespoons (12 grams) potato starch
1 teaspoon (5 grams) xanthan gum

• In a small bowl, combine all the ingredients. Store in an airtight container until ready to use.

Leavening

Raised doughnuts use yeast as their primary leavening agent. All the yeast-raised doughnut recipes in this book call for active dry yeast; if you are using fresh cake yeast, you'll need to double the quantity listed in each recipe. If you think you'll be making yeast-raised doughnuts fairly regularly, it's far more cost effective to buy active dry yeast in bulk rather than in individual packages; store this quantity of yeast in the refrigerator.

Baking powder and, for some recipes, baking soda provide leavening for cake doughnuts. Whenever baking powder is called for in a recipe, it's best to use an aluminum-free double-acting baking powder.

A NOTE ON PROOFING: Yeast doughs have to rest for a while to let the yeast do its business and aerate the dough; this makes the doughnuts soft and light and develops the flavor. The basic yeast (raised) dough recipe (page 2) has three separate proofing stages. The first is creating a soft "sponge," which jump-starts the yeast into action. The second is a longer rise, done either in a warm environment (70 to 80 degrees F) or in the refrigerator, depending on the recipe. The third and final stage occurs after the dough has been rolled and cut. In this stage, the temperature of the dough and the room can have a big impact on how long it takes to achieve the right amount of rise, so the time needed can vary considerably; keep a close eye on the dough, checking at five-minute intervals. When properly proofed, the doughnut rings will be quite puffy and rounded, but still springy.

Cake doughnuts don't need to proof, but they do need a resting period to give the flour a chance to absorb the liquid. Without this rest, cake doughnuts can take up too much oil from the fryer and become heavy and greasy.

Sugar

These recipes are best made using superfine sugar, which melts into the dough smoothly and works beautifully to coat the doughnuts, after frying, with a quick shake in a bag. If you are using regular granulated sugar, which is less dense than superfine, follow the weight measurements or heap your volume measurements.

Fats and oils

Fat incorporated into the dough helps prevent the dough from absorbing too much oil while frying, so don't be tempted to skimp. Solid fats like coconut oil, vegetable shortening, lard, or unsalted butter work best. Liquid fats tend to run out of the doughnut, leaving a greasy mess once the doughnut has cooled.

For deep-frying, I recommend safflower oil, which is inexpensive and very heat tolerant. Peanut oil is another great choice if you are cooking for those without nut allergies. Canola oil and sunflower oil are also good choices.

How much oil you need will depend on the size of your pot. You should fill the pot with a depth of at least two inches of oil and leave at least two inches from the top of the oil to the top of the pot.

You can use the same frying oil several times, but it is important to strain out any particles between uses and to change the oil completely if it starts to get dark or if your doughnuts are starting to feel too greasy on the surface even when cooked at the right temperature. Old oil leads to greasy, off-tasting doughnuts.

When you are done with the oil, make sure you dispose of it properly according to your city's regulations. Do not pour it down the drain, or you may find yourself quickly racking up plumbing expenses! If you compost, you can stir small amounts of oil in with other organic material. Most cities have residential cooking oil drop-off locations, where the used oil is recycled into biodiesel. You might also check with local restaurants to see whether you can add your used oil to their grease bins.

And of course, deep-frying should always be done with caution. Never leave a pot of oil heating on the stove unattended!

TOOLS
. . . .

Here are a few tools that will make your doughnut making easier.

Doughnut cutters

All you really need is a biscuit cutter (or even an upside-down glass) to make doughnuts, but a doughnut cutter that cuts the holes out at the same time is a nice little gadget to have and should run you only about six dollars. Make sure you get one that is made from very firm metal and doesn't bend easily as some cookie cutters do.

A large, heavy-bottomed pot

Even though I own a deep fryer, I prefer to use a small three-quart Dutch oven to fry doughnuts. It uses less oil, and cleanup is a bit easier. Just make sure your pot is deep enough to hold at least two inches of oil with at least two inches of clearance to the top of the pot.

A fast, accurate thermometer

If you are frying on the stove top, a fast, accurate thermometer that can measure up to 400 degrees F is a must-have. Look for one that is labeled a deep-fat or candy thermometer. You can also use laser thermometers, and follow the manufacturer's instructions. Make sure yours is working properly with this simple test: Bring a pot of water to a boil on the stove. Meanwhile, fill a glass with ice water. Now stick the thermometer in the ice water (you may not be able to get a reading if your thermometer doesn't go that low; that's OK). When the water comes to a boil, move the thermometer to the boiling water, being careful not to touch the tip to the bottom of the pan. Pay attention to how long it takes to come up to 212 degrees F. If it takes more than thirty seconds, consider getting a faster thermometer.

A stand mixer with a dough hook attachment

It's certainly possible to make any dough in this book without a stand mixer and a dough hook, but if you have one, you should use it. You can make the doughs by hand—and skip your upper-arm workout at the gym. Using a hand mixer or even mixing with a wooden spoon is fine for any of the cake doughs but not recommended where a dough hook is specifically called for.

A dough bucket

If you are making raised dough, a plastic dough bucket with volume markings on the side will help you know more easily when your dough has doubled in size.

A pastry cloth

I've found that the best material on which to place rising yeast doughnuts—without getting the dough stuck to it—is either linen or a tight-weave, non-terry cloth towel, well dusted with flour. You can also use parchment paper during the proofing stage, but the dough may stick a bit. If it does, try greasing the paper with some cooking spray before placing the doughnuts on it.

A pastry bag and parchment paper

Some doughnuts are lighter and fluffier when made from a batter instead of a shape-able dough. Professional doughnut shops use a special doughnut dropper to make perfect rings that drop directly into the hot oil. Inexpensive versions are also available online, but they don't work as well with this book's cake recipes as simply using a pastry bag to pipe the batter onto little squares of greased parchment, and then drop-ping the doughnut, parchment and all, into the oil. The parchment will slide off easily once the doughnut has started to brown. (For full details on this technique, see Basic Cake, page 20).

For filled doughnuts, a needlelike Bismarck (#230) tip works best to inject the filling without creating too much of a hole. A star tip will work in a pinch.

A nut milk bag

If you are making your own almond milk (page 73) or coconut milk (page 75) for glazes, a nut milk bag is the best way to filter out the creamy liquid from the gritty meat. If you don't have one, you can use a double layer of cheesecloth.

Doughnut pans

If you are baking cake doughnuts, you'll need to buy a special doughnut pan with a rounded cup and post in the middle for each doughnut. Without one, your cake doughnuts will spread and have very flat, hard bottoms. You don't need a special pan for baking raised doughnuts, though. Although the bottoms will be slightly flatter than that of their fried counterparts, it's barely noticeable.

Doughnut machines

There are all sorts of electric gadgets for making mini doughnuts. You don't need any of them to make doughnuts at home, but they certainly make for some fun party entertainment.

For even more on doughnuts, visit my blog at DoughnutCookbook.com.

DOUGHS

BASIC RAISED

The quintessential doughnut: fluffy, sweet, heavenly. There's nothing like a still-warm raised doughnut to bring a smile to your face. This basic dough recipe is very subtly sweet, so you can glaze away with your favorite flavors and not worry about the doughnuts getting cloying. This updated version is less yeasty than my original recipe but just as fluffy.

MAKES 8 TO 12 DOUGHNUTS | ACTIVE TIME: 25 MINUTES | READY IN: 3 HOURS

1 tablespoon plus 1 teaspoon active dry yeast, divided

1 cup whole milk, heated to 110 degrees F, divided

2 to 3 cups (240 to 360 grams) bread flour, divided, plus more for dusting

3 egg yolks, at room temperature

1 teaspoon vanilla extract

2 tablespoons super-fine sugar

½ teaspoon kosher salt

¼ cup (½ stick) unsalted butter or vegetable short-ening, at room temperature

Vegetable oil for frying

• In a medium bowl, dissolve 1 table-spoon of the yeast in ¾ cup of the milk. Add ¾ cup of the flour and stir to create a smooth paste. Cover the bowl with plastic wrap and let it rest in a warm spot for 30 minutes.

• In the bowl of a stand mixer fitted with the paddle attachment, combine the remaining ¼ cup milk and 1 teaspoon yeast with a spoon. Add the rested flour mixture, egg yolks, and vanilla. Mix on medium speed until smooth. Turn off

the mixer and add 1 cup of the flour, the sugar, and salt. Mix on low speed for about 30 seconds or until the dough starts to come together. Add the butter and mix on medium speed until incorporated, about 30 seconds.

• Switch to the dough hook attachment. With the mixer turned off, add more flour, about ¼ cup at a time, and knead the dough on medium speed between additions, until the dough pulls com-pletely away from the sides of the bowl and is smooth. It will be very soft and moist, but not so sticky that you can't roll it out. You may have flour left over. Cover the bowl with plastic wrap and let it sit in a warm spot for 30 minutes. Gently degas the dough and refrigerate for at least 1 hour (and up to 12 hours).

• Line a baking sheet with a lightly floured non–terry cloth dish towel. Roll out the dough on a lightly floured surface to ½ inch thick. With a doughnut or cookie cutter, cut out 3-inch rounds with 1-inch holes (for filled doughnuts, don't cut out the holes).

• Place the doughnuts on the prepared baking sheet at least 1 inch apart and cover with plastic wrap. Let them sit in a warm spot to proof until almost doubled in size, 30 to 40 minutes, testing at 5-minute intervals. To test whether the dough is ready, touch it lightly with a fingertip. If it springs back immediately, it needs more time. If it springs back slowly, it is ready. If it doesn't spring back at all, it has overproofed; you can punch it down and reroll and reproof it for another 30 minutes once.

• While the doughnuts are proofing, in a heavy-bottomed pot, heat at least 2 inches of oil until a deep-fat thermometer registers 360 degrees F. With a metal spatula, carefully put the doughnuts in the oil. Fry for 1 to 2 minutes on each side, or until light golden brown. Remove with a slotted spoon, drain on a wire rack set over a paper towel, and let cool slightly before glazing or filling.

NOTE: Have leftover dough scraps? Make doughnut bread! Just knead the scraps together and put in a greased brioche pan, or form into rolls and put in a muffin tin. Brush the tops of the dough with milk or melted butter, cover with plastic wrap, and let sit in a warm spot for 15 minutes. Preheat the oven to 425 degrees F, and bake for about 12 minutes, or until deep brown on top. Let the bread cool on a wire rack for at least 10 minutes.

BAKED RAISED

Most baked sweet doughs end up more like bagels than doughnuts, but these, based on a Finnish sweet dough recipe, are so soft and light you may not realize they were baked. A quick dip in glaze will keep the crust from becoming too chewy, but they are still best eaten straight away.

MAKES 10 TO 14 DOUGHNUTS | ACTIVE TIME: 20 MINUTES | READY IN: 2 HOURS

1 egg, at room temperature

¼ cup (60 grams) superfine sugar

1 cup whole milk, heated to 110 degrees F

1 tablespoon active dry yeast

2 teaspoons vanilla extract

1 teaspoon kosher salt

2½ to 3½ cups (300 to 420 grams) all-purpose flour, divided, plus more for dusting

½ cup (1 stick) unsalted butter, cut into 1-inch cubes, at room temperature

Vegetable oil for greasing

• In the bowl of a stand mixer fitted with the paddle attachment, beat the egg and sugar on medium speed until blended, about 1 minute. Add the milk, yeast, vanilla, and salt and mix on medium speed to blend. With the mixer on low speed, add 2 cups of the flour about ½ cup at a time, and beat until the dough is thick and pulls away from the sides of the bowl, about 2 minutes.

• Switch to the dough hook attachment. With the mixer on medium speed, add the butter one piece at a time, and beat until no large chunks are left in the bottom of the bowl, 3 to 5 minutes. Reduce the speed to low and add additional flour until the dough gathers around the hook and pulls completely away from the sides of the bowl. It will be soft and moist, but not overly sticky. You may have flour left over.

• Turn the dough out onto a floured surface and knead gently until the dough no longer sticks to your hands. Lightly grease a large mixing bowl. Transfer the dough to the bowl and turn to coat. Cover with a damp tea towel or plastic wrap and let rise in a warm spot until doubled in size, about 1 hour.

• Punch down the dough and roll out to ½ inch thick, lightly flouring the surface if the dough sticks. With a doughnut or cookie cutter, cut out 3-inch rounds with 1-inch holes (for filled doughnuts, don't cut out the holes).

• Preheat the oven to 400 degrees F and line a baking sheet with parchment paper. Place the doughnuts at least 1 inch apart on the baking sheet. Cover with plastic wrap and let them sit in a warm spot until nearly doubled in size, about 20 minutes.

• Bake until the doughnuts are a light golden brown, 5 to 8 minutes, being very careful not to overbake them. Immediately glaze them, or brush with butter and dust with superfine sugar, and eat while still warm.

GLUTEN-FREE BASIC RAISED

Didn't think you could have raised doughnuts anymore because you can't tolerate gluten? Think again. These gluten-free raised doughnuts may not be exactly like Krispy Kremes, but I think they'll satisfy the craving.

MAKES 8 TO 12 DOUGHNUTS | ACTIVE TIME: 20 MINUTES | READY IN: 2 HOURS

2 to 3 cups Gluten-Free Baking Mix for Yeast Doughnuts (page xi)

½ tablespoon baking powder

1½ tablespoons active dry yeast, divided

3 tablespoons super-fine sugar

¾ cup whole milk, heated to 110 degrees F

2 eggs, at room temperature

1 egg white, at room temperature

2 tablespoons unsalted butter or vegetable shortening, at room temperature

1 teaspoon vanilla extract

1 teaspoon apple cider vinegar

½ teaspoon kosher salt

Tapioca starch for dusting

Vegetable oil for greasing and frying

• In a medium bowl, whisk the baking mix and baking powder.

• In the bowl of a stand mixer fitted with the paddle attachment, dissolve the yeast and sugar in the milk. Add 1 cup of the baking mix and mix on low speed to create a thick paste. Add the eggs, egg white, butter, vanilla, vinegar, and salt and mix on medium speed for 1 minute.

• Switch to the dough hook attachment. With the mixer turned off, add the remaining baking mix about ¼ cup at a time, and knead the dough on medium speed between additions, until the dough starts to pull away from the sides of the bowl and form a ball, 1 to 2 minutes. It will be very soft and moist, but not so sticky that you can't roll it out. You may have baking mix left over.

• With lightly greased hands, form the dough into a ball and put it in a large ziplock bag. Let it rest in a warm spot for 30 minutes.

• Roll out the dough on a lightly floured surface to ½ inch thick. With a doughnut or cookie cutter, cut out 3-inch rounds with 1-inch holes (for filled doughnuts, don't cut out the holes).

• Line a baking sheet with a lightly floured non-terry cloth dish towel. Place the doughnuts at least 1 inch apart on the baking sheet and cover with plastic wrap. Let them sit in a warm spot until they are nicely rounded on top, about 45 minutes.

• While the doughnuts are proofing, in a heavy-bottomed pot, heat at least 2 inches of oil until a deep-fat thermometer registers 340 degrees F. With a metal spatula, carefully put the doughnuts in the oil. Don't overfill the pot. Fry for 1 to 2 minutes on each side, or until light golden brown. Remove with a slotted spoon, drain on a wire rack set over a paper towel, and let cool slightly before glazing or filling.

VEGAN RAISED

No animal products are required in this superlight and fluffy raised dough.

MAKES 8 TO 12 DOUGHNUTS | ACTIVE TIME: 25 MINUTES | READY IN: 3 HOURS

1 tablespoon plus 1 teaspoon active dry yeast, divided

1 cup almond milk (or milk of choice), heated to 110 degrees F, divided

2 to 3 cups (240 to 360 grams) bread flour, divided

2 tablespoons potato starch

1 teaspoon vanilla extract

2 tablespoons super-fine sugar

½ teaspoon kosher salt

¼ cup coconut oil or vegetable shortening, melted

Vegetable oil for frying

• In a medium bowl, dissolve 1 tablespoon of the yeast in ¾ cup of the milk. Add ¾ cup of the flour and stir to create a smooth paste. Cover the bowl with plastic wrap and let it rest in a warm spot for 30 minutes.

• In the bowl of a stand mixer fitted with the paddle attachment, combine the remaining ¼ cup milk and 1 teaspoon yeast with a spoon. Add the rested flour mixture, potato starch, and vanilla. Mix on low speed until smooth. Turn off the mixer and add 1 cup of the flour, the sugar, and salt. Mix on low speed for about 30 seconds or until the dough starts to come together. Add the coconut oil and mix on medium speed until incorporated, about 30 seconds.

• Switch to the dough hook attachment. With the mixer turned off, add more flour, about ¼ cup at a time, and knead the dough on medium speed between additions, until the dough pulls completely away from the sides of the bowl and is smooth. It will be very soft and moist, but not so sticky that you can't roll it out. You may have flour left over. Cover the bowl with plastic wrap and let it sit in a warm spot for 30 minutes. Gently degas the dough and refrigerate for at least 1 hour (and up to 12 hours).

• Roll out and cut the doughnuts, let rise, and fry as directed for Basic Raised doughnuts (page 2).

CHOCOLATE RAISED

Most chocolate doughnuts in bakeries are cake doughnuts. But for the true chocoholic, try this raised dough, which brings a fun chocolaty twist to basic raised doughnuts. Use Dutch processed cocoa powder for the most chocolaty flavor.

MAKES 8 TO 12 DOUGHNUTS | ACTIVE TIME: 25 MINUTES | READY IN: 3 HOURS

1 tablespoon plus 1 teaspoon active dry yeast, divided

1 cup whole milk, heated to 110 degrees F, divided

2 to 3 cups (240 to 360 grams) bread flour, divided

3 egg yolks, at room temperature

⅓ cup (28 grams) Dutch processed cocoa powder

1 teaspoon vanilla extract

¼ cup (60 grams) superfine sugar

½ teaspoon baking soda

½ teaspoon kosher salt

¼ cup (½ stick) unsalted butter or vegetable shortening, at room temperature

Vegetable oil for frying

• In a medium bowl, dissolve 1 tablespoon of the yeast in ¾ cup of the milk. Add ¾ cup of the flour and stir to create a smooth paste. Cover the bowl with plastic wrap and let it rest in a warm spot for 30 minutes.

• In the bowl of a stand mixer fitted with the paddle attachment, combine the remaining ¼ cup milk and 1 teaspoon yeast on low speed. Add the rested flour mixture, egg yolks, cocoa powder, and vanilla. Mix on medium speed until smooth. Turn off the mixer and add 1 cup of the flour, the sugar, baking soda, and salt. Mix on low speed for about 30 seconds or until the dough starts to come together. Add the butter and mix on low speed until incorporated, about 30 seconds.

• Switch to the dough hook attachment. With the mixer turned off, add more flour, about ¼ cup at a time, and knead the dough on medium speed between additions, until the dough pulls completely away from the sides of the bowl and is smooth. It will be very soft and moist, but not so sticky that you can't roll it out. You may have flour left over. Cover the bowl with plastic wrap and let it sit in a warm spot for 30 minutes. Gently degas the dough and refrigerate for at least 1 hour (and up to 12 hours).

• Roll out and cut the doughnuts, let rise, and fry as directed for Basic Raised doughnuts (page 2).

SOURDOUGH RAISED

Sourdough in raised doughnuts helps create an even more flavorful and fluffy dough with a little less yeast than traditional raised doughnuts. The sourdough starter does take some upkeep, but I think it's well worth the babysitting for the extra boost to flavor it can provide for any of your baked goods, from breads to waffles to, of course, these doughnuts!

MAKES 8 TO 12 DOUGHNUTS | ACTIVE TIME: 25 MINUTES | READY IN: 4 HOURS

2 tablespoons Sourdough Starter (recipe follows)

2 to 3 cups (240 to 360 grams) bread flour, divided

¼ cup water

½ cup whole milk, heated to 110 degrees F

2 teaspoons active dry yeast

3 egg yolks, at room temperature

1 teaspoon vanilla extract

2 tablespoons super-fine sugar

½ teaspoon kosher salt

¼ cup (½ stick) unsalted butter or vegetable short-ening, at room temperature

Vegetable oil for frying

• In a medium bowl, combine the sour-dough starter, ¼ cup of the flour, and the water. Stir to create a wet paste. Cover the bowl with plastic wrap and let it rest at room temperature for at least 1 hour (2 hours if the sourdough starter was cold to begin with), or up to 12 hours.

• After the sourdough has rested, in the bowl of a stand mixer fitted with the paddle attachment, combine the milk and yeast on low speed. Add the sour-dough mixture, egg yolks, and vanilla.

Mix on low speed until smooth. Turn off the mixer and add 1 cup of the flour, the sugar, and salt. Mix on low speed for about 30 seconds or until the dough starts to come together. Add the butter and mix on medium speed until incor-porated, about 30 seconds.

• Switch to the dough hook attachment. With the mixer turned off, add more flour, about ¼ cup at a time, and knead the dough on medium speed between addi-tions, until the dough pulls completely away from the sides of the bowl and is smooth. It will be very soft and moist, but not so sticky that you can't roll it out. You may have flour left over. Cover the bowl with plastic wrap and let it sit in a warm spot until doubled in size, 1 to 2 hours. Gently degas the dough and refrigerate for at least 1 hour (and up to 12 hours).

• Roll out and cut the doughnuts, let rise, and fry as directed for Basic Raised doughnuts (page 2).

CONTINUED . . .

Sourdough Starter

MAKES 1 TO 2 CUPS OF STARTER

Day 1

1 cup (120 grams) rye flour

½ cup water (filtered if possible)

2 tablespoons pineapple juice

Days 2 through 5

½ cup (60 grams) all-purpose flour (or flour of choice)

½ cup water (filtered if possible)

• On day 1, in a glass container with a lid, mix the rye flour, water, and pineapple juice until all the flour has been moistened. Loosely cover and keep at room temperature, ideally around 70 degrees F.

• On day 2, you will likely not notice much change, but it's time to feed the starter. Remove and discard about half of the mixture (½ to 1 cup), and stir in the all-purpose flour and water. Mix well, loosely cover, and keep at room temperature.

• Repeat the feeding process for the next 3 days. The starter should begin to smell tangy (but not rotten), look bubbly, and grow in size. If the starter has not risen or does not look bubbly after day 5, continue to repeat the feeding process for an additional 3 days.

• Once the starter has become active, refrigerate it and reduce the feeding process to once a week.

SAVORY WHOLE WHEAT RAISED

Not all doughnuts have to be sweet! This savory whole wheat version may completely change your expectations of what a doughnut should be. Make them your own with your choice of savory spices and herbs.

MAKES 8 TO 12 DOUGHNUTS | ACTIVE TIME: 25 MINUTES | READY IN: 3 HOURS

1 tablespoon plus 1 teaspoon active dry yeast, divided

1 cup whole milk, heated to 110 degrees F, divided

1½ cups (180 grams) bread flour, divided

1 cup (120 grams) rye flour

¾ cup (90 grams) whole wheat flour

3 egg yolks, at room temperature

1 teaspoon savory herbs or dried aromatics, such as caraway, rosemary, or dried onion

1 tablespoon super-fine sugar

½ teaspoon kosher salt

¼ cup (½ stick) unsalted butter or vegetable short-ening, at room temperature

Vegetable oil for frying

2 tablespoons unsalted butter, melted

Flaky sea salt, sesame seeds, poppy seeds, or other toppings for garnish

• In a medium bowl, dissolve 1 table-spoon of the yeast in ¾ cup of the milk. Add 1 cup of the bread flour and stir to create a smooth paste. Cover the bowl with plastic wrap and let it rest in a warm spot for 30 minutes.

• In a small bowl, mix the remaining ½ cup bread flour, the rye flour, and whole wheat flour.

• In the bowl of a stand mixer fitted with the paddle attachment, combine the remaining ¼ cup milk and 1 tea-spoon yeast with a spoon. Add the rested flour mixture, egg yolks, and herbs. Mix on low speed until smooth. Turn off the mixer and add 1 cup of the combined flours, the sugar, and salt. Mix on low speed for about 30 sec-onds or until the dough starts to come together. Add the butter and mix on medium speed until incorporated, about 30 seconds.

• Switch to the dough hook attachment. With the mixer turned off, add more flour, about ¼ cup at a time, and knead the dough on medium speed between additions, until the dough pulls com-pletely away from the sides of the bowl and is smooth. It will be very soft and moist, but not so sticky that you can't roll it out. You may have flour left over. Cover the bowl with plastic wrap and let it sit in a warm spot for 30 minutes. Gently degas the dough and refrigerate for at least 1 hour (and up to 12 hours).

CONTINUED . . .

• Roll out and cut the doughnuts, let rise, and fry as directed for Basic Raised doughnuts (page 2).

• Brush the top of each doughnut with melted butter, and sprinkle with toppings like flaky sea salt, sesame seeds, or whatever you might like on a bagel.

NOTE: Want your savory doughnuts a bit lighter, like their sweet cousins? Switch out half of the rye flour and all of the whole wheat flour with an equal amount of bread flour.

MALASADAS

Malasadas are small yeast doughnuts, usually cut square, that originated in Portugal and became very popular in Hawaii, where they are served hot and dusted with sugar or filled with custard or fruit preserves.

MAKES 12 TO 20 *MALASADAS* | ACTIVE TIME: 30 MINUTES | READY IN: 3 HOURS

2 tablespoons luke-warm water

1 tablespoon active dry yeast

½ cup (120 grams) superfine sugar, divided, plus more for dusting

3 eggs, at room temperature

2 tablespoons unsalted butter or vegetable shortening, melted

½ cup whole milk, at room temperature

½ cup half-and-half, at room temperature

¼ teaspoon kosher salt

3 to 4 cups (360 to 480 grams) bread flour

Vegetable oil for frying

• In a small bowl, sprinkle the water with the yeast and 1 teaspoon of the sugar. Stir and let sit until foamy, about 5 minutes.

• In the bowl of a stand mixer fitted with the paddle attachment, beat the eggs on medium speed until thick. Add the yeast mixture, the remaining sugar, the butter, milk, half-and-half, and salt. Mix on low speed until just combined.

• Switch to the dough hook attachment. With the mixer turned off, add more flour about ½ cup at a time, and knead the dough on medium speed between additions, until the dough pulls completely away from the sides of the bowl and is smooth. The dough will be moist, but not too sticky. You may have flour left over.

• Cover the dough with plastic wrap and let it rise in a warm spot until doubled in size, about 1 hour. Flip the dough over, cover, and let rise until doubled in size again, about 1 hour.

• In a heavy-bottomed pot, heat at least 2 inches of oil until a deep-fat thermometer registers 350 degrees F.

• Roll out the dough on a lightly floured surface to ½ inch thick, then with a knife cut it into 2-inch squares. For more rustic-looking *malasadas*, you can just pinch off small balls of the unrolled dough and press them flat between your palms.

• With a metal spatula, carefully put the doughnuts in the oil. Fry for 1 to 2 minutes on each side, or until golden. Remove with a slotted spoon and drain briefly on a paper towel. Fill a paper bag with sugar, add the doughnuts, and shake. Serve immediately.

BASIC CAKE

Making these subtly spiced cake doughnuts is so easy and quick. They are the perfect pairing with coffee, in the morning or even for dessert.

MAKES 8 TO 12 TRADITIONAL DOUGHNUTS OR 25 TO 35 DROP DOUGHNUTS
ACTIVE TIME: 15 MINUTES | READY IN: 40 MINUTES

2 cups (240 grams) all-purpose flour, sifted

⅓ cup (80 grams) superfine sugar

2 teaspoons baking powder

½ teaspoon kosher salt

½ teaspoon freshly grated nutmeg or ground allspice

2 tablespoons unsalted butter or vegetable shortening, at room temperature

½ cup whole milk, scalded and cooled, divided

1 egg, at room temperature

2 tablespoons plain yogurt, at room temperature

1 teaspoon vanilla extract

Vegetable oil for greasing and frying

• In the bowl of a stand mixer fitted with the paddle attachment, combine the flour, sugar, baking powder, salt, and nutmeg. Blend on low speed. Add the butter and blend at medium-low speed until the mixture resembles coarse sand.

• In a small bowl, combine ¼ cup of the milk, the egg, yogurt, and vanilla. With the mixer on medium speed, slowly pour the wet ingredients into the flour mixture. Scrape down the sides of the bowl and mix for 20 seconds. Add the remaining ¼ cup milk, a little at a time, until the batter sticks to the sides of the bowl. The batter should be smooth, thick, and pipeable, similar to moist cookie dough. You may not need all of the milk. Cover with plastic wrap and let rest for 15 to 20 minutes.

• In a heavy-bottomed pot, heat at least 2 inches of oil until a deep-fat thermometer registers 360 degrees F.

• For traditional doughnuts, spoon the batter into a pastry bag fitted with a ⅓-inch round tip. Determine how many 3-inch doughnuts can fry in your pot at one time without crowding. Grease a 4-inch parchment square for each doughnut and pipe a 3-inch-diameter ring onto each square. Carefully put one in the oil, parchment side up. Remove the parchment with tongs and repeat with a few more rings, being careful not to over-fill the pan. Fry for 1 to 2 minutes on each side, or until light golden brown.

• For drop doughnuts, drop tablespoon-size dollops directly into the oil, being careful not to overfill the pan, and fry for about 45 seconds on each side, or until light golden brown.

• Remove with a slotted spoon and drain on a paper towel. Repeat with the remaining batter. Let cool just slightly before glazing and eating.

NOTE: To scald milk, place the milk in a heavy-bottomed pot over medium heat, stirring occasionally until the milk reaches 180 degrees F. The surface of the milk will be steamy and a bit foamy. Continue to cook for about 15 seconds, and remove from heat and cool at room temperature for about 5 minutes.

BAKED CAKE

Cake doughnuts are fried, not baked, at your local doughnut shop. But this recipe bakes up just as delicious, not to mention a bit less guilt inducing, and cleanup is far easier. This batter also turns out beautifully in an electric doughnut maker.

MAKES 8 TO 12 DOUGHNUTS | ACTIVE TIME: 15 MINUTES | READY IN: 30 MINUTES

1 cup (120 grams) all-purpose flour

¼ cup (30 grams) whole wheat pastry flour

1 teaspoon baking powder

⅓ cup (80 grams) superfine sugar

½ teaspoon freshly grated nutmeg or ground allspice

½ teaspoon kosher salt

2 tablespoons unsalted butter or vegetable short-ening, at room temperature

1 egg, beaten, at room temperature

¼ cup whole milk, scalded and cooled

¼ cup plain yogurt, at room temperature

1 teaspoon vanilla extract

Vegetable oil for greasing

• Preheat the oven to 350 degrees F. Lightly grease a doughnut pan.

• In a large bowl, sift the flours and baking powder. Whisk in the sugar, nutmeg, and salt. Add the butter and use your clean fingers to rub it into the dry ingredients as you would when making a pastry crust, until evenly distributed and butter chunks are smaller than pea-size.

Add the egg, milk, yogurt, and vanilla, and stir until just combined. Do not over-mix or your doughnuts may be rubbery.

• Use a pastry bag or a spoon to fill each doughnut cup about three-quarters full, making sure the center post is clear. Bake until the doughnuts are a light golden brown and spring back when touched, 6 to 10 minutes. Let them cool slightly before removing from the pan and glazing.

NOTE: To get the proper doughnut shape when baking cake doughnuts, you do need a doughnut pan (see page xvi). Baking them on a flat baking sheet will result in flat-bottomed half doughnuts. If you don't have a dough-nut pan, you can bake this batter in a muffin tin for classic-doughnut-flavored muffins. The batter also works great with a mini-muffin tin for bite-size treats.

GLUTEN-FREE CAKE

These lightly spiced cake doughnuts are a real treat for those who can't tolerate gluten in their diet.

MAKES 8 TO 12 TRADITIONAL DOUGHNUTS OR 25 TO 35 DROP DOUGHNUTS
ACTIVE TIME: 15 MINUTES | READY IN: 40 MINUTES

2 cups (280 grams) Gluten-Free Baking Mix for Cake Doughnuts (page xi)

⅓ cup (80 grams) superfine sugar

1 tablespoon baking powder

½ teaspoon guar gum

½ teaspoon kosher salt

½ teaspoon freshly grated nutmeg or ground allspice

¼ cup (½ stick) unsalted butter or vegetable shortening, at room temperature

2 eggs, separated, at room temperature

⅔ cup whole milk, scalded and cooled

¼ cup plain yogurt, at room temperature

2 teaspoons vanilla extract

Vegetable oil for frying

Pinch of cream of tartar

• In the bowl of a stand mixer fitted with the paddle attachment, combine the baking mix, sugar, baking powder, guar gum, salt, and nutmeg. Blend on low speed. Add the butter and blend on medium-low speed until the mixture resembles coarse sand.

• In a small bowl, combine the egg yolks, milk, yogurt, and vanilla. With the mixer on medium speed, slowly pour the wet ingredients into the baking mixture. Scrape down the sides of the bowl and mix for 30 seconds. The batter should be smooth, thick, and pipeable, similar to moist cookie dough. Cover the bowl with a towel or plastic wrap. Let rest for 15 to 20 minutes.

• In a heavy-bottomed pot, heat at least 2 inches of oil until a deep-fat thermometer registers 350 degrees F.

• Either by hand in a medium bowl or with the whisk attachment of a stand mixer, whisk the egg whites and cream of tartar until soft peaks form. Fold the egg whites into the rested batter. Pipe and fry the doughnuts as directed for Basic Cake doughnuts (page 20).

....

VARIATION: For a chocolate version, add ¼ cup (15 grams) unsweetened natural cocoa powder, ½ teaspoon baking soda, and an additional 2 tablespoons superfine sugar to the baking mixture.

VEGAN CAKE

In the first edition of this book, this recipe included guar gum to help replace the function of eggs in the batter. It worked, and the doughnuts were good, but gums are expensive and aren't used in the kitchen very often. Then I discovered aquafaba, that oft-discarded bean water that comes in a can of chickpeas, whips up into perfect vegan meringues.

MAKES 8 TO 12 TRADITIONAL DOUGHNUTS OR 25 TO 35 DROP DOUGHNUTS
ACTIVE TIME: 15 MINUTES | READY IN: 40 MINUTES

2 cups (240 grams) all-purpose flour, sifted

⅓ cup (80 grams) superfine sugar

2 teaspoons baking powder

½ teaspoon kosher salt

½ teaspoon freshly grated nutmeg or ground allspice

2 tablespoons coconut oil or vegetable shortening, at room temperature

½ cup almond milk, scalded and cooled, divided

3 tablespoons strained aquafaba, at room temperature

2 tablespoons plain soy yogurt, at room temperature

1 teaspoon vanilla extract

Vegetable oil for greasing and frying

• In the bowl of a stand mixer fitted with the paddle attachment, combine the flour, sugar, baking powder, salt, and nutmeg, and blend on low speed. Add the coconut oil and blend on medium-low speed until the mixture resembles coarse sand.

• In a small bowl, mix ¼ cup of the milk, the aquafaba, yogurt, and vanilla. With the mixer on medium speed, slowly pour the wet ingredients into the flour mixture. Scrape down the sides of the bowl and mix for 20 seconds. Add the remaining ¼ cup milk, a little at a time, until the batter sticks to the sides of the bowl. The batter should be smooth, thick, and pipeable, similar to moist cookie dough. You may not need all of the milk. Cover the dough with plastic wrap and let rest for 15 to 20 minutes.

• Pipe and fry the doughnuts as directed for Basic Cake doughnuts (page 20)

....

VARIATION: For a chocolate version, add ¼ cup (15 grams) unsweetened natural cocoa powder, ½ teaspoon baking soda, and an additional 2 tablespoons superfine sugar to the flour mixture.

CHOCOLATE CAKE

These rich chocolate cake doughnuts are a bit more chocolaty than the doughnuts you find in chain doughnut stores, which, let's face it, are more brown than chocolate. If you prefer them less chocolaty, you can reduce the amount of cocoa powder to ¼ cup. If you use Dutch processed cocoa powder, use half the amount of baking soda.

MAKES 8 TO 12 DOUGHNUTS | ACTIVE TIME: 15 MINUTES | READY IN: 40 MINUTES

2 cups (240 grams) all-purpose flour, sifted

½ cup (120 grams) superfine sugar

⅓ cup (27 grams) unsweetened natural cocoa powder

½ tablespoon baking powder

½ teaspoon baking soda

½ teaspoon kosher salt

2 tablespoons unsalted butter or vegetable shortening, at room temperature

1 egg, at room temperature

½ cup whole milk, scalded and cooled

2 tablespoons plain yogurt, at room temperature

1 teaspoon vanilla extract

Vegetable oil for frying

• In the bowl of a stand mixer fitted with the paddle attachment, combine the flour, sugar, cocoa powder, baking powder, baking soda, and salt, and blend on low speed. Add the butter and blend on medium-low speed until the mixture resembles coarse sand.

• In a small bowl, combine the egg, milk, yogurt, and vanilla. With the mixer on medium speed, slowly pour the wet ingredients into the flour mixture. Scrape down the sides of the bowl and mix for 30 seconds. The batter should be smooth, thick, and not too wet, similar to sugar cookie dough. Cover the bowl with a towel or plastic wrap. Let the dough rest for 15 to 20 minutes.

• In a heavy-bottomed pot, heat at least 2 inches of oil until a deep-fat thermometer registers 360 degrees F.

• Roll out the dough on a generously floured surface to ½ inch thick. With a doughnut or cookie cutter, cut out 3-inch rounds with 1-inch holes. Brush off any excess flour.

• With a metal spatula, carefully put the doughnuts in the oil. Fry for 1 to 2 minutes on each side. Remove with a slotted spoon and drain on a paper towel. Let cool just slightly before glazing.

SOURDOUGH CAKE

A little sourdough starter in your cake doughnuts gives a nice tang and tenderness to these quick-to-make doughnuts.

MAKES 8 TO 12 TRADITIONAL DOUGHNUTS OR 25 TO 35 DROP DOUGHNUTS
ACTIVE TIME: 15 MINUTES | READY IN: 40 MINUTES (with active sourdough starter)

2 cups (240 grams) all-purpose flour, sifted

⅓ cup (80 grams) superfine sugar

2 teaspoons baking powder

½ teaspoon kosher salt

½ teaspoon freshly grated nutmeg or allspice

¼ cup Sourdough Starter (page 14)

2 tablespoons unsalted butter or vegetable shortening, at room temperature

1 egg, at room temperature

2 tablespoons whole milk, at room temperature

2 tablespoons plain yogurt, at room temperature

1 teaspoon vanilla extract

1 to 4 tablespoons water

Vegetable oil for greasing and frying

• In the bowl of a stand mixer fitted with the paddle attachment, combine the flour, sugar, baking powder, salt, and nutmeg. Blend on low speed. Add the sourdough starter and butter and blend on medium-low speed until the mixture resembles coarse sand.

• In a small bowl, combine the egg, milk, yogurt, and vanilla. With the mixer on medium speed, slowly pour the wet ingredients into the flour mixture. Scrape down the sides of the bowl and mix for 20 seconds. Add water, 1 tablespoon at a time, until the batter sticks to the sides of the bowl. The batter should be smooth, thick, and pipeable, similar to moist cookie dough. Cover with a towel or plastic wrap and let rest for 30 minutes.

• Pipe and fry the doughnuts as directed for Basic Cake doughnuts (page 20).

OLD-FASHIONED SOUR CREAM

What's the difference between a cake doughnut and an old-fashioned? The two are sibling pastries. Cake doughnuts are the straitlaced ones; old-fashioned, contrary to the name, are a bit on the wild side. As they fry, they split and crack all over the place, making a crisp crust with all sorts of crags to catch glaze and frosting flavors.

MAKES 8 TO 12 DOUGHNUTS | ACTIVE TIME: 15 MINUTES | READY IN: 40 MINUTES

1¼ cups (150 grams) all-purpose flour

1 teaspoon baking soda

½ teaspoon ground cinnamon, nutmeg, or allspice

Pinch of kosher salt

⅓ cup (80 grams) superfine sugar

¼ cup sour cream, at room temperature

1 egg, at room temperature

1 tablespoon unsalted butter or vegetable shortening, at room temperature

Vegetable oil for frying

• In a small bowl, sift the flour, baking soda, and cinnamon. Stir in the salt.

• In a medium bowl, whisk the sugar, sour cream, egg, and butter until smooth. Add the flour mixture, a little at a time, and stir until a smooth dough forms. Cover the bowl with plastic wrap and refrigerate the dough for 15 to 20 minutes.

• Roll out the dough on a lightly floured surface to about ½ inch thick. With a doughnut or cookie cutter, cut out 2½-inch rounds with ½-inch holes. You can reroll any scrap dough.

• Fry as directed for Chocolate Cake doughnuts (page 28).

RICOTTA

This quick and easy batter yields plenty of the fluffiest fritters you've ever tasted.

MAKES 10 TO 14 TRADITIONAL DOUGHNUTS OR 25 TO 35 DROP DOUGHNUTS
ACTIVE TIME: 20 MINUTES | READY IN: 20 MINUTES

1½ cups (180 grams) all-purpose flour

2 teaspoons baking powder

¼ cup (60 grams) superfine sugar

3 eggs, at room temperature

8 ounces ricotta cheese, at room temperature

1 tablespoon freshly grated lemon zest

1 teaspoon vanilla extract

Vegetable oil for frying

Confectioners' sugar, or 1 batch Honey glaze (page 62) for finishing

• In a medium bowl, sift the flour and baking powder. Stir in the superfine sugar, eggs, ricotta, lemon zest, and vanilla, mixing just enough to combine. Do not overmix. Use the batter immediately or refrigerate, covered with plastic wrap, for up to 1 day.

• Pipe and fry the doughnuts as directed for Basic Cake doughnuts (page 20).

• Sprinkle with confectioners' sugar or drizzle with glaze.

APPLE CIDER

A little bit of graham flour makes these doughnuts a bit nuttier and helps them fry up with a wonderfully crisp, nubby crust. However, feel free to replace the graham flour with all-purpose for a more traditional apple cider doughnut.

MAKES 10 TO 14 DOUGHNUTS | ACTIVE TIME: 15 MINUTES | READY IN: 40 MINUTES

1¾ cups (210 grams) all-purpose flour

¼ cup (30 grams) graham flour

2 teaspoons ground cinnamon

2 teaspoons baking powder

1 teaspoon baking soda

½ teaspoon kosher salt

2 tablespoons unsalted butter or vegetable short-ening, at room temperature

½ cup (120 grams) superfine sugar

2 egg yolks, at room temperature

¼ cup apple cider, at room temperature

¼ cup buttermilk, at room temperature

1 teaspoon vanilla extract

Vegetable oil for frying

• In a small bowl, whisk the flours, cinnamon, baking powder, baking soda, and salt.

• In the bowl of a stand mixer fitted with the paddle attachment, cream the butter and sugar on low speed. Add the egg yolks and beat on medium speed until the mixture is fluffy and pale yellow, about 3 minutes. Using a wooden spoon, stir in the cider, buttermilk, and vanilla. Add the dry ingredients and stir just until the mixture comes together to create a soft, slightly sticky dough. Cover with plastic wrap and refrigerate for 15 to 20 minutes.

• Roll out the dough on a lightly floured surface to about ½ inch thick. With a doughnut or cookie cutter, cut out 2½-inch rounds with ½-inch holes. You can reroll any scrap dough.

• In a heavy-bottomed pot, heat at least 2 inches of oil until a deep-fat thermometer registers 360 degrees F. With a metal spatula, carefully put the doughnuts in the oil, being careful not to overcrowd the pot. Fry until they turn a rich golden brown, about 1 minute on each side. Remove with a slotted spoon and drain on a paper towel. Repeat with the remaining dough. Let cool to the touch before glazing and eating.

NOTE: You can bake these dough-nuts in a doughnut pan, in a 350-degree-F oven for 5 to 10 minutes, but you won't achieve the same rich golden color.

ALE CAKE

Adding a bit of bubbly to your cake doughnut batter helps make the crumb both lighter and crisper, due to the carbon dioxide and alcohol.

MAKES 8 TO 12 TRADITIONAL DOUGHNUTS OR 25 TO 35 DROP DOUGHNUTS
ACTIVE TIME: 15 MINUTES | READY IN: 40 MINUTES

2 cups (240 grams) all-purpose flour, sifted

⅓ cup (80 grams) superfine sugar

2 teaspoons baking powder

½ teaspoon kosher salt

½ teaspoon freshly grated nutmeg or ground allspice

2 tablespoons unsalted butter or vegetable short-ening, at room temperature

1 egg, at room temperature

½ cup ale of choice or hard cider, divided

2 tablespoons plain yogurt, at room temperature

1 teaspoon vanilla extract

Vegetable oil for frying

• In the bowl of a stand mixer fitted with the paddle attachment, combine the flour, sugar, baking powder, salt, and nutmeg. Blend on low speed. Add the butter and blend on medium-low speed until the mixture resembles coarse sand.

• In a small bowl, combine the egg, ¼ cup of the ale, the yogurt, and vanilla. With the mixer on medium speed, slowly pour the wet ingredients into the flour mixture. Scrape down the sides of the bowl and mix for 20 seconds. Add the remaining ¼ cup ale, a little at a time, until the batter sticks to the sides of the bowl. The batter should be smooth, thick, and pipeable, similar to moist cookie dough. You may not need all of the ale. Cover with plastic wrap and let rest for 15 to 20 minutes.

• Pipe and fry the doughnuts as directed for Basic Cake doughnuts (page 20).

CROISSANT DOUGHNUTS

Dominique Ansel's Cronut had hungry New York pastry lovers lining up for hours for the doughnut-croissant hybrid. For my version of the many-layered pastry, I've riffed on the laminated dough used in the cinnamon roll (one of my favorites) at Seattle's Macrina Bakery. While the dough takes a couple of days to make, most of the time involves waiting in between dough rests . . . it's less time consuming than waiting for hours in line!

MAKES 16 TO 20 DOUGHNUTS | ACTIVE TIME: 1 HOUR | READY IN: 2 DAYS

Day 1

1½ cups whole milk

1½ tablespoons active dry yeast

3 tablespoons super-fine sugar

1 tablespoon vanilla extract

3 cups (360 grams) bread flour

½ tablespoon kosher salt

Day 2

1½ cups (3 sticks) unsalted butter, chilled

3 tablespoons bread flour, plus more for dusting

Vegetable oil for frying

1 batch glaze of choice

1 batch filling of choice, if using

• On day 1, in a small saucepan over medium heat, heat the milk until it is warm to the touch. Don't overheat! Transfer to a large bowl and add the yeast, sugar, and vanilla and gently stir. Let it sit for about 5 minutes until bubbly.

• In a small bowl, combine the flour and salt, mixing with a wooden spoon. Slowly add the flour mixture to the milk mixture and stir until just combined. The dough will be sticky. Cover the dough with plastic wrap and refrigerate for 8 to 12 hours.

• On day 2, remove the dough from the refrigerator and punch it down.

• Cut the butter into 12 equal pieces. In the bowl of a stand mixer fitted with the paddle attachment, mix the butter and 3 tablespoons flour on low speed until the butter is completely smooth. Scoop the butter mixture onto a well-floured surface and shape into a 6-inch square about 1 inch or so thick. This is called a butter block. Lightly flour the square and wrap it in plastic wrap. Refrigerate both the dough and the butter block for about 30 minutes. You want them to be about the same temperature before proceeding.

• Line a baking sheet with parchment paper and set aside.

• Now it's time to work the butter into the dough. On a well-floured surface, gently pat the dough into a square about 1 inch thick, then stretch the corners out about 4 inches to make a sort of X shape. Place the butter block in the center and fold the stretched corners over the butter. Pinch the edges of the dough together to completely seal the butter inside. Sprinkle the dough with a bit of flour and gently roll it out into a 12-by-20-inch rectangle. If the butter starts to poke through, pinch the dough to reseal it.

• Next, position the rectangle so that a long side is closest to you. Take the left side and fold it to the center. Fold the right side over to meet it, then fold the new left edge over the new right edge as if you are closing a book. Carefully lift the dough onto the prepared baking sheet. Cover with plastic wrap and refrigerate for 30 minutes.

• Remove the dough from the refrigerator and let sit at room temperature for 15 minutes. Repeat the rolling, folding, and chilling process two more times, for a total of three book folds and three chills. The last chill can be 30 minutes to 12 hours.

CONTINUED . . .

• Remove the dough from the refrigerator and cut it in half. Place one half on a lightly floured surface and return the other half, covered with plastic wrap, to the refrigerator.

• Line a baking sheet with a lightly floured non-terry cloth dish towel. Roll out the dough half to ½ inch thick. With a doughnut or cookie cutter, cut out 2½-inch rounds with 1-inch holes, and place them at least 1½ inches apart on the prepared baking sheet. Cover them with plastic wrap and repeat with the other half of the dough.

• To use dough scraps, form them into a rectangle and perform a book fold, then refrigerate for 15 minutes before rolling and cutting them. Or, even better, create cinnamon roll doughnuts (see Note).

• Let the doughnuts sit in a warm spot (70 to 80 degrees F) for 1 hour, or until doubled in size.

• While the doughnuts are proofing, in a heavy-bottomed pot, heat at least 2 inches of oil until a deep-fat thermometer registers 360 degrees F. With a metal spatula, carefully put the doughnuts in the oil. Fry for about 1 minute on each side, or until light golden brown. Remove with a slotted spoon, and drain on a wire rack set over a paper towel and cool to the touch before filling or glazing.

NOTE: To make cinnamon roll doughnuts from dough scraps, roll the chilled dough into a rectangle and sprinkle with a bit of granulated sugar and ground cinnamon. Roll the dough into a tube and cut the tube into ½-inch slices. Line a baking sheet with a lightly floured non-terry cloth dish towel, and set the slices on the towel. Cover with plastic wrap and let rise for 1 hour. Fry the doughnuts in 350-degree-F oil until they are a deep golden brown, 1 to 2 minutes on each side. You may need to fry them longer than you would normal doughnuts so that they cook all the way through. Test the first one to make sure it doesn't have a raw center.

• To fill the doughnuts, spoon the filling into a pastry bag with a Bismarck (#230) tip. Insert the tip into the bottom of a doughnut in four equally spaced spots. Gently squeeze the pastry bag to add about 1 tablespoon filling, withdrawing the tip slowly as you squeeze. Repeat with the remaining doughnuts.

• Glaze as desired.

FRENCH CRULLERS

There are two kinds of crullers: hand-twisted cake doughnuts, which are more akin to maple bars, and French crullers made with pâte à choux, which are lighter than air, with all sorts of nooks and crannies to hold onto their light honey glaze. These crullers, one of my family's favorites, are the latter.

MAKES 10 TO 14 CRULLERS | ACTIVE TIME: 30 MINUTES | READY IN: 30 MINUTES

1 cup water

6 tablespoons unsalted butter

2 teaspoons superfine sugar

¼ teaspoon kosher salt

1 cup (120 grams) all-purpose flour, sifted

3 eggs, at room temperature

2 egg whites, slightly beaten, at room temperature

Vegetable oil for greasing and frying

1 batch Honey glaze (page 62) or glaze of choice

• In a heavy-bottomed pot over medium-high heat, combine the water, butter, sugar, and salt and bring to a brisk boil. Add the flour and stir with a wooden spoon until completely incorporated. Cook, stirring, for 3 to 4 minutes to steam away as much water as possible. The more moisture you can remove, the more eggs you can add later and the lighter your pastry will be. The mixture is ready when a thin film coats the bottom of the pan.

• Transfer the mixture to the bowl of a stand mixer fitted with the paddle attachment. (Although you can mix the pâte à choux by hand, this can be rather arduous, so use a mixer if you have one.) Stir the mixture on low speed for about 1 minute to allow it to cool. Increase the speed to medium and add 1 egg. Mix until it is completely incorporated, then scrape down the sides of the bowl. Add the remaining eggs, one at a time, mixing in each completely before adding the next. Add the egg whites, a little at a time, and mix until the paste becomes smooth and glossy and holds a slight peak when pinched with your fingers. Be careful not to add too much egg white or your crullers will become heavy; you may have some left over. Spoon the batter into a pastry bag fitted with a ½-inch star tip.

NOTE: Undercooked crullers will collapse while cooling, so observe the first one and if this happens, increase the frying time (and check the oil temperature) for the rest.

- In a heavy-bottomed pot, heat at least 2 inches of oil until a deep-fat thermometer registers 370 degrees F. Cut out 12 (3-inch) squares of parchment paper and lightly grease them. Pipe a ring onto each square. When the oil is hot, place one cruller at a time in the oil, parchment side up. Remove the parchment with tongs. Fry them 1 to 2 minutes on each side, or until golden brown. Remove with a slotted spoon and drain on a paper towel for at least 1 minute. Once cool to the touch, the crullers can be glazed.

....

VARIATION: Crullers also bake very well, although they will have slightly firmer crusts than the fried versions. Preheat the oven to 450 degrees F. Line a baking sheet with parchment paper and pipe the crullers onto it, at least 2 inches apart. Bake for 5 minutes, then reduce the heat to 350 degrees F and bake for another 15 minutes. Turn off the heat, open the oven door slightly, and let the crullers sit in the cooling oven for 10 minutes. Remove from the oven, dip in the glaze, and cool on a wire rack until the glaze has set.

NOTE: Beignets, the classic New Orleans fried dough treats, use this same batter and are even easier to prepare. Simply drop rounded teaspoonfuls of the batter into the oil. As the dough puffs, the beignets will turn themselves over—but keep an eye on them and flip any that need a little help. Once cooled, sprinkle with a little confectioners' sugar, toss in a bag of superfine granulated sugar, or drizzle with a chocolate glaze.

GHANAIAN DOUGHNUTS

While there are many different versions of Ghanaian doughnuts, this is the version I fell in love with. These little dough balls puff by the same magic as cream puffs, but when fried, they are the best combination of crispy crust and custardy inside. The coarser sanding sugar covering these doughnuts is reminiscent of the beaches on which these doughnuts are commonly found, but you can use any sugar you like or serve with a tropical fruit jam.

**MAKES 20 TO 25 DROP DOUGHNUTS | ACTIVE TIME: 30 MINUTES
READY IN: 30 MINUTES**

½ cup plus 2 table-spoons water

½ cup whole milk

½ cup (1 stick) unsalted butter, cut into pieces

2 tablespoons sweet-ened condensed milk

½ teaspoon kosher salt

1 cup (120 grams) all-purpose flour

3 eggs, at room temperature

1 egg white, at room temperature

¼ cup sanding sugar

• In a heavy-bottomed pot over medium-high heat, combine the water, whole milk, butter, sweetened condensed milk, and salt and bring to a brisk boil. Add the flour and stir with a wooden spoon until completely incorporated. Cook, stirring, for 3 to 4 minutes to steam away as much water as possible. The more moisture you can remove, the more eggs you can add later and the lighter your pastry will be. The mixture is ready when a thin film coats the bottom of the pan.

• Transfer the mixture to the bowl of a stand mixer fitted with the paddle attachment. (Although you can mix the dough by hand, this can be rather arduous, so use a mixer if you have one.) Stir the mixture on low speed for about 1 minute to allow it to cool. Increase the speed to medium and add 1 egg. Mix until it is completely incorporated, then scrape down the sides of the bowl. Add the remaining eggs, one at a time, mixing in each completely before adding the next. Add the egg white, a little at a time, until the paste becomes smooth and glossy and holds a slight peak when pinched with your fingers. Be careful not to add too much egg white or your doughnuts may become heavy. You may not use it all.

• Place the sanding sugar in a shallow bowl or a paper bag, and set aside.

• In a heavy-bottomed pot, heat at least 2 inches of oil until a deep-fat thermometer registers 355 degrees F. When the oil is hot, drop heaping teaspoonfuls of the batter into the oil. Be careful not to overfill the pot. Fry for 1 to 2 minutes on each side, or until light golden brown.

Remove with a slotted spoon and drain on a wire rack set over a paper towel for at least 1 minute, and then roll in or shake with the sanding sugar. They are lovely served warm.

SPANISH CHURROS

These churros are based on the traditional Spanish style, which are made without eggs (versus Mexican-style churros, which are made with a dough similar to the one used for French Crullers, page 44) and have a crunchy crust with a creamy center. It's best to make them on the small side, using a smaller piping tip, to ensure the center cooks through.

MAKES 12 TO 15 CHURROS | ACTIVE TIME: 15 MINUTES | READY IN: 30 MINUTES

1 cup (120 grams) all-purpose flour, sifted

1 teaspoon kosher salt

1 tablespoon olive oil

1½ cups boiling water, divided

Vegetable oil for greasing and frying

2 tablespoons super-fine sugar

1 tablespoon ground cinnamon

Chocolate Sauce (recipe follows) or Homemade Dulce de Leche (page 156)

• In a large bowl, combine the flour and salt. Pour the olive oil and 1 cup of the boiling water on top. Stir the dough with a wooden spoon until the mixture is well combined and resembles mashed potatoes, 1 to 2 minutes. If the dough seems too stiff to pipe, add a bit more water. Cover the bowl with a towel and let rest for 10 minutes.

• In a small bowl, mix the sugar and cinnamon.

• Spoon the dough into a pastry bag fitted with a ¼-inch star tip. Squeeze the dough down to remove any pockets.

• Heat at least 2 inches of vegetable oil in a heavy-bottomed pot until a deep-fat thermometer registers 360 degrees F. Cut out 3 (8-by-3-inch) pieces of parchment paper and lightly grease them. Pipe a 4-inch strip of dough onto each parchment piece. When the oil is hot, put the strips in the oil one at a time, parchment side up. Remove the parchment with tongs. Fry on each side until the oil starts to bubble frantically and the churros are golden brown, 2 to 3 minutes total, flipping each one once or twice. Remove with tongs and drain on a wire rack set over a paper towel for about 30 seconds. Sprinkle with the cinnamon-sugar mixture. Repeat with the remaining dough (you can reuse the parchment strips).

• Serve the churros warm with the chocolate sauce or warmed dulce de leche.

Chocolate Sauce

MAKES ABOUT 1 CUP

⅔ cup heavy cream

2½ ounces bitter-
sweet or semisweet
chocolate, coarsely
chopped

1 teaspoon cornstarch

Pinch of kosher salt

• In a small pot over low heat, heat the cream until steaming. Remove from the heat and stir in the chocolate, cornstarch, and salt. Whisk until the chocolate has completely melted and the mixture is smooth.

SOPAPILLAS

Unlike the crisp, cinnamon-sugar-and-whipped-cream-covered triangles you find in many Tex-Mex restaurants, these New Mexico–style *sopapillas* are like little pillows of dough and air. Serve a basket of them in place of tortillas alongside a big bowl of *chile verde*; offer them again for dessert with a drizzle of honey.

MAKES 6 TO 12 *SOPAPILLAS* | ACTIVE TIME: 20 MINUTES | READY IN: 40 MINUTES

2½ cups (300 grams) all-purpose flour, plus more for dusting

1 teaspoon baking powder

1 teaspoon kosher salt

2 tablespoons vegetable shortening or lard

⅔ cup warm water

Vegetable oil for frying

• In a medium bowl, sift the flour, baking powder, and salt. Add the shortening and gently work it in with your clean fingertips until the mixture resembles coarse crumbs. Add the water, a little at a time, and mix with a fork until the dough forms a ball. Turn it out onto a lightly floured surface and knead for about 30 seconds. Cover with plastic wrap and let rest for 30 minutes.

• In a heavy-bottomed pot, heat at least 2 inches of oil until a deep-fat thermometer registers 370 degrees F.

• On a lightly floured surface, roll out the dough very thin, ⅛ to ¼ inch thick. Cut into 3-inch squares or triangles.

• With a metal spatula, carefully put them in the oil and fry until golden and puffed, 1 to 2 minutes on each side. Only fry a couple at a time to avoid overfilling the pot. Remove with a slotted spoon and drain on a paper towel, allowing to cool just slightly.

NOTE: *Sopapillas* are best eaten immediately but can be kept warm in a 200-degree-F oven for up to 1 hour.

LOUKOUMADES

I first learned of these puffy little fritters, a traditional treat on the island of Cyprus, in Tessa Kiros's beautiful cookbook *Falling Cloudberries.* The honey syrup is amazing too.

MAKES 20 TO 30 *LOUKOUMADES* | ACTIVE TIME: 30 MINUTES | READY IN: 3 HOURS

½ tablespoon active dry yeast

¾ cup lukewarm water

¾ cup (90 grams) all-purpose flour, divided

Pinch of superfine sugar

Pinch of kosher salt

1 large baking potato (about 8 ounces), peeled and halved

¼ cup honey

2 tablespoons freshly squeezed lemon juice

¼ teaspoon ground cinnamon

Splash of water

Vegetable oil for frying

• In the bowl of a stand mixer fitted with the paddle or dough attachment, combine the yeast and water. Stir to distribute the yeast. Add ¼ cup of the flour, the sugar, and salt. Stir again, cover the bowl with plastic wrap, and let sit for 20 minutes in a warm spot.

• Boil the potato until easily pierced with a fork, 10 to 15 minutes. Drain, let cool, and mash well.

• Add the potato and the remaining ½ cup flour to the yeast mixture. Beat on high speed to form a smooth, wet dough. Cover the bowl with plastic wrap and let sit in a warm spot until the batter has thickened, about 2 hours.

• Meanwhile, make the syrup. In a medium heavy-bottomed pot over medium-low heat, stir the honey, lemon juice, cinnamon, and water. Boil until the mixture thickens, about 10 minutes. Set aside.

• In a heavy-bottomed pot, heat at least 2 inches of oil until a deep-fat thermometer registers 360 degrees F. Drop in heaping teaspoonfuls of batter and fry, turning occasionally, until golden and puffed, about 1 minute. Remove with a slotted spoon. Drain on a paper towel and let cool slightly.

• To serve, place the *loukoumades* in a bowl and drizzle with the syrup.

PICARONES

Picarones are sweet, ring-shaped winter squash fritters enjoyed in Peru. Traditionally they are sweetened with *miel de chancaca*, a sweet sauce made of raw cane sugar and honey and flavored with orange. A good sour and sweet marmalade is a simpler and equally delicious substitute.

MAKES 6 TO 12 *PICARONES* | ACTIVE TIME: 30 MINUTES | READY IN: 2 HOURS

½ stick cinnamon

4 whole cloves

2 tablespoons whole aniseed

1 medium yam (3 ounces), peeled and halved

4 ounces pumpkin or winter squash, peeled and cut into 3-inch chunks

2 teaspoons active dry yeast

1 teaspoon superfine sugar

Pinch of kosher salt

1½ to 2 cups (200 to 240 grams) all-purpose flour

Vegetable oil for frying

Miel de chancaca or marmalade for serving

• Bring a large pot of water to a boil. Add the cinnamon, cloves, and aniseed and simmer for 10 minutes. Strain out the spices and discard them, keeping the spiced water. Add the yam and pumpkin to the water and simmer until soft, about 10 minutes.

• Reserve 2 tablespoons of the cooking water in a small bowl, discarding the rest, and let it cool to about 110 degrees F. Add the yeast and sugar and let sit for 5 minutes.

• In the bowl of a stand mixer fitted with the paddle attachment, put the yam and pumpkin and beat on medium speed to a smooth puree. Stir in the salt and the yeast mixture. Beat on high speed until smooth. Reduce the speed to low, and add the flour, a little at a time, until a soft, elastic dough forms. If the dough is still sticky, add a bit more flour.

• Cover the dough with plastic wrap and proof in a warm spot until doubled in size, about 1 hour.

• In a heavy-bottomed pot, heat at least 2 inches of oil until a deep-fat thermometer registers 360 degrees F. Pinch off golf ball–size pieces of dough and shape them into rings with your fingers. With a metal spatula, carefully put the rings in the oil and fry 1 to 2 minutes on each side, or until golden. Remove with a slotted spoon, drain on a paper towel, and let cool slightly before serving with the *miel de chancaca* or marmalade on the side.

GLAZES & TOPPINGS

BASIC SUGAR

This is the classic doughnut glaze, which works well with any sort of doughnut. Using milk gives a slight opaqueness to the glaze but doesn't affect the flavor.

MAKES ENOUGH FOR A STANDARD DOUGHNUT RECIPE
ACTIVE TIME: 5 MINUTES | READY IN: 5 MINUTES

1½ cups (180 grams) confectioners' sugar, sifted

Pinch of kosher salt

2 teaspoons vanilla extract (optional)

3 to 4 tablespoons milk of choice or water

- In a medium bowl, combine the sugar and salt and slowly stir in the vanilla and milk, a little at a time, to make a smooth, pourable glaze. You may not use all of the milk.

- Dip the top of each doughnut in the glaze, gently shaking to remove any excess. For an allover glaze, flip and dip the other side as well. Allow the glaze to set, 5 to 10 minutes.

CHOCOLATE

You can make this chocolate dip as chocolaty as you'd like by adjusting the ratio of powdered sugar to cocoa powder. Or try dark cocoa powder for an even more intense chocolate flavor.

MAKES ENOUGH FOR A STANDARD DOUGHNUT RECIPE
ACTIVE TIME: 5 MINUTES | READY IN: 5 MINUTES

1½ cups (180 grams) confectioners' sugar

¼ cup (27 grams) unsweetened natural cocoa powder

2 tablespoons milk of choice or water

2 teaspoons vanilla extract

• In a medium bowl, sift the sugar and cocoa powder. Slowly stir in the milk and vanilla, a little at a time, to make a smooth, pourable glaze. You may not use all of the milk.

• Dip the top of each doughnut in the glaze, gently shaking to remove any excess. Allow the glaze to set, 5 to 10 minutes.

HONEY

Try different honey types in this glaze for subtly different flavors—from light and bright orange blossom to dark avocado honey that has hints of raisin.

MAKES ENOUGH FOR A STANDARD DOUGHNUT RECIPE
ACTIVE TIME: 5 MINUTES | READY IN: 5 MINUTES

1½ cups (180 grams) confectioners' sugar, sifted

Pinch of kosher salt

1 tablespoon honey

3 to 4 tablespoons milk of choice or water

• In a medium bowl, combine the sugar and salt and slowly stir in the honey and milk, a little at a time, to make a smooth, pourable glaze. You may not use all of the milk.

• Dip the top of each doughnut in the glaze, gently shaking to remove any excess. For an allover glaze, flip and dip the other side as well. Allow the glaze to set, 5 to 10 minutes.

MAPLE

While you should definitely try this maple glaze on Apple Cider doughnuts (page 36) and Maple-Bacon Bars (page 180), it's really a safe go-to on just about any doughnut you want glazed.

MAKES ENOUGH FOR A STANDARD DOUGHNUT RECIPE
ACTIVE TIME: 5 MINUTES | READY IN: 5 MINUTES

1½ cups (180 grams) confectioners' sugar, sifted

Pinch of kosher salt

2 tablespoons maple syrup

2 tablespoons milk of choice or water

• In a medium bowl, combine the sugar and salt, and slowly stir in the syrup and milk, a little at a time, to make a smooth, pourable glaze. You may not use all of the milk.

• Dip the top of each doughnut in the glaze, gently shaking to remove any excess. For an allover glaze, flip and dip the other side as well. Allow the glaze to set, 5 to 10 minutes.

CITRUS

Lemon, lime, and orange definitely make a tasty, tangy glaze, but don't forget to try other varieties like blood orange, sour orange, pomelo, or even kumquat!

MAKES ENOUGH FOR A STANDARD DOUGHNUT RECIPE
ACTIVE TIME: 5 MINUTES | READY IN: 5 MINUTES

1½ cups (180 grams) confectioners' sugar, sifted

Pinch of kosher salt

3 to 4 tablespoons freshly squeezed citrus juice

• In a medium bowl, combine the sugar and salt, and slowly stir in the citrus juice, a little at a time, to make a smooth, pourable glaze. You may not use all of the juice.

• Dip the top of each doughnut in the glaze, gently shaking to remove any excess. For an allover glaze, flip and dip the other side as well. Allow the glaze to set, 5 to 10 minutes.

CINNAMON SPICE

Cinnamon with allspice is my favorite spice combination for this glaze, but it's also delicious with a bit of nutmeg, cardamom, or even a smidge of black pepper.

MAKES ENOUGH FOR A STANDARD DOUGHNUT RECIPE
ACTIVE TIME: 5 MINUTES | READY IN: 5 MINUTES

1½ cups (180 grams) confectioners' sugar, sifted

Pinch of kosher salt

½ teaspoon ground cinnamon

½ teaspoon ground allspice

3 to 4 tablespoons milk of choice or water

• In a medium bowl, combine the sugar and salt, and whisk in the cinnamon and allspice. Slowly stir in the milk, a little at a time, to make a smooth, pourable glaze. You may not use all of the milk.

• Dip the top of each doughnut in the glaze, gently shaking to remove any excess. For an allover glaze, flip and dip the other side as well. Allow the glaze to set, 5 to 10 minutes.

BROWN BUTTER

Brown butter may just be the elixir that solves all the world's problems. Or at least it makes a pretty amazing doughnut glaze.

MAKES ENOUGH FOR A STANDARD DOUGHNUT RECIPE
ACTIVE TIME: 15 MINUTES | READY IN: 15 MINUTES

3 tablespoons unsalted butter

1½ cups (180 grams) confectioners' sugar, sifted

Pinch of kosher salt

1 to 2 tablespoons milk of choice or water

• In a heavy-bottomed pan over medium-low heat, cook the butter until the solids separate and begin to brown, about 10 minutes. Remove from the heat immediately.

• In a medium bowl, combine the sugar and salt, and slowly stir in the brown butter and milk, a little at a time, to make a smooth, pourable glaze. This glaze will quickly firm up, so use it while it is still warm or reheat for 10 to 20 seconds in the microwave before using.

• Dip the top of each doughnut in the glaze, gently shaking to remove any excess. For an allover glaze, flip and dip the other side as well. Allow the glaze to set, 5 to 10 minutes.

BOURBON

Top-shelf bourbons, like Four Roses or Blanton's, meld sweet and strong into a smooth sip and bring a delicious complexity to this boozy glaze.

MAKES ENOUGH FOR A STANDARD DOUGHNUT RECIPE
ACTIVE TIME: 5 MINUTES | READY IN: 5 MINUTES

1½ cups (180 grams) confectioners' sugar, sifted

Pinch of kosher salt

2 to 3 tablespoons top-shelf bourbon

2 teaspoons vanilla extract

• In a medium bowl, combine the sugar and salt, and slowly stir in the bourbon and vanilla, a little at a time, to make a smooth, pourable glaze. You may not use all of the bourbon.

• Dip the top of each doughnut in the glaze, gently shaking to remove any excess. For an allover glaze, flip and dip the other side as well. Allow the glaze to set, 5 to 10 minutes.

CARAMEL

This frosting brings a bite of caramel flavor in a fraction of the time it would take to make a true caramel.

MAKES ENOUGH FOR A STANDARD DOUGHNUT RECIPE
ACTIVE TIME: 10 MINUTES | READY IN: 10 MINUTES

¼ cup whole milk

2½ tablespoons unsalted butter

¼ cup brown sugar

¼ cup (60 grams) superfine sugar

¼ teaspoon sea salt

½ cup (60 grams) confectioners' sugar

1 teaspoon vanilla extract (optional)

• In a heavy-bottomed pot over medium heat, combine the milk, butter, brown and superfine sugars, and salt and cook for 3 minutes, stirring occasionally. Remove from the heat and let cool.

• In the bowl of a stand mixer fitted with the paddle attachment, sift the confectioners' sugar into the cooled caramel. Beat on medium speed until incorporated. Add the vanilla and beat on low speed until smooth.

• Use an offset spatula to spread the frosting on each doughnut. Serve immediately.

GINGER

Bottled ginger juice packs even more gingery spice into this glaze, but if you can't find it, just double the amount of ground ginger.

MAKES ENOUGH FOR A STANDARD DOUGHNUT RECIPE
ACTIVE TIME: 5 MINUTES | READY IN: 5 MINUTES

1½ cups (180 grams) confectioners' sugar, sifted

Pinch of kosher salt

½ teaspoon ground ginger

1 teaspoon ginger juice

3 to 4 tablespoons milk of choice or water

• In a medium bowl, combine the sugar and salt, and whisk in the ground ginger. Slowly stir in the ginger juice and milk, a little at a time, to make a smooth, pourable glaze. You may not use all of the milk.

• Dip the top of each doughnut in the glaze, gently shaking to remove any excess. For an allover glaze, flip and dip the other side as well. Allow the glaze to set, 5 to 10 minutes.

BERRY

For a fun and flavorful glaze, make it with berries! Raspberries and strawberries will create a beautiful pink glaze, while blueberries and blackberries will be almost purple.

MAKES ENOUGH FOR A STANDARD DOUGHNUT RECIPE
ACTIVE TIME: 15 MINUTES | READY IN: 30 MINUTES

½ cup berries of choice, fresh or frozen

1 tablespoon freshly squeezed lemon juice

1 tablespoon water

1½ cups (180 grams) confectioners' sugar, sifted

Milk of choice or water for thinning

• In a small pot over medium-low heat, combine the berries, lemon juice, and water, and bring to a simmer. Stir, smashing the berries as they soften. Continue to stir and simmer until the berries have completely broken down, about 10 minutes. Remove from the heat and push the berry mash through a fine-mesh sieve, discarding the solids. Set aside to cool for about 15 minutes.

• In a medium bowl, slowly stir the cooled berry juice into the sugar, a little at a time, until you have a smooth, pour-able glaze. You may not need all of the juice. If needed, you can add a little bit of milk or water to thin the glaze further.

• Dip the top of each doughnut in the glaze, gently shaking to remove any excess. For an allover glaze, flip and dip the other side as well. Allow the glaze to set, 5 to 10 minutes.

ALMOND

Making homemade almond milk for this glaze takes a bit of preplanning, since the nuts need to soak for 8 to 12 hours. You can use store-bought almond milk, but the homemade version will be more almondy.

MAKES ENOUGH FOR A STANDARD DOUGHNUT RECIPE
ACTIVE TIME: 5 MINUTES | READY IN: 5 MINUTES

1½ cups (180 grams) confectioners' sugar, sifted

Pinch of kosher salt

¼ teaspoon almond extract

3 to 4 tablespoons Homemade Almond Milk (recipe follows) or store-bought

• In a medium bowl, combine the sugar and salt. Slowly stir in the almond extract and milk, a little at a time, until you have a smooth, pourable glaze.

• Dip the top of each doughnut in the glaze, gently shaking to remove any excess. For an allover glaze, flip and dip the other side as well. Allow the glaze to set, 5 to 10 minutes.

Homemade Almond Milk

MAKES 3 TO 4 CUPS | ACTIVE TIME: 10 MINUTES | READY IN: 8½ TO 12½ HOURS

1 cup raw peeled slivered almonds

7 to 8 cups water, divided

• Put the almonds in a quart jar and fill it with water (up to 4 cups). Cover the jar with a lid or plastic wrap and let it sit for 8 to 12 hours. Drain the almonds and discard the water.

• Put the softened almonds in a high-powered blender, and add 2 cups of water. Blend until you can no longer see pieces of almond, about 3 minutes. Add another cup of water and blend 1 minute more. For thinner milk, add up to another cup of water. Strain the milk through a fine-mesh sieve or a nut milk bag, and refrigerate the almond milk in an airtight container for up to 4 days.

COCONUT

Making your own coconut milk for this glaze requires learning an essential desert island skill: learning how to open a whole coconut. But don't worry. It's easier to do than you might think . . . there are lots of tutorials online. Store-bought coconut milk makes a delicious glaze too. I recommend using the type found in the refrigerated section of grocery stores, which is meant for drinking, versus canned coconut milk, which is meant for cooking.

MAKES ENOUGH FOR A STANDARD DOUGHNUT RECIPE
ACTIVE TIME: 5 MINUTES | READY IN: 5 MINUTES

1½ cups (180 grams) confectioners' sugar, sifted

Pinch of kosher salt

3 to 4 tablespoons Homemade Coconut Milk (recipe follows) or store-bought

• In a medium bowl, combine the sugar and salt. Shake the coconut milk to emulsify it, and slowly stir it, a little at a time, into the sugar mixture, until you have a smooth, pourable glaze.

• Dip the top of each doughnut in the glaze, gently shaking to remove any excess. For an allover glaze, flip and dip the other side as well. Allow the glaze to set, 5 to 10 minutes.

Homemade Coconut Milk

MAKES ABOUT 1 CUP | ACTIVE TIME: 15 MINUTES | READY IN: 15 MINUTES

1 cup fresh coconut meat

1¼ cups fresh coconut water or tap water, or a combination

• In a high-powered blender, put the coconut and ¼ cup of the coconut water. Blend until no large pieces remain. Add the remaining cup of water and blend well, until the milk is as smooth as possible, about 3 minutes.

• Place a nut milk bag over a large jar and strain the coconut milk through the bag, squeezing well to extract as much liquid as possible.

• As the coconut milk sits, the thick coconut cream will rise to the top. You can emulsify room-temperature coconut milk simply by shaking it (cold coconut milk may not emulsify). Refrigerate the coconut milk in an airtight container for up to 4 days.

CANDY SPRINKLES

It takes a huge amount of patience to wait for these colorful sprinkles to dry, but be sure not to rush them or you'll end up with mushy goo. The sprinkles will keep well in an airtight container for months, but the color may fade a little.

MAKES ABOUT ⅓ CUP | ACTIVE TIME: 20 MINUTES | READY IN: 24 HOURS

1½ cups (180 grams) confectioners' sugar, sifted

3 tablespoons pasteurized egg white

1 teaspoon vanilla or other extract

¼ teaspoon fine salt

Assorted natural food colorings

• In a small bowl, mix the sugar, egg white, vanilla, and salt to create a smooth paste. Divide the paste into different containers if you would like to make different colors. Add the food coloring and blend well.

• Spoon the paste into a pastry bag fitted with a very small plain tip. Line a baking sheet with parchment paper.

• For a classic sprinkle shape, pipe teeny-tiny lines on the prepared baking sheet, leaving at least ½ inch of space between each one. Let dry at room temperature for 24 hours, then slice into your preferred size of sprinkle.

• For dots, pipe teeny-tiny dots onto the prepared baking sheet, leaving ½ inch between each dot. Let dry at room temperature for 24 hours before using.

CHOCOLATE SPRINKLES

These chocolate sprinkles aren't the super shiny versions you can buy in the store, but they are more chocolaty. Also try these with dark chocolate cocoa powder!

MAKES ABOUT ⅓ CUP | ACTIVE TIME: 20 MINUTES | READY IN: 24 HOURS

1½ cups (180 grams) confectioners' sugar, sifted

½ cup (50 grams) unsweetened natural cocoa powder

2 tablespoons water, plus more as needed

1 teaspoon vanilla extract

¼ teaspoon fine salt

• In a small bowl, mix the sugar, cocoa powder, water, vanilla, and salt to create a shiny paste, adding a bit more water if needed.

• Spoon the paste into a pastry bag fitted with a very small plain tip. Line a baking sheet with parchment paper.

• For a classic shape, pipe teeny-tiny lines along the prepared baking sheet, leaving at least ½ inch of space between each one. Let dry at room temperature for 24 hours, then slice into your preferred size of sprinkle.

• For dots, pipe teeny-tiny dots onto the prepared baking sheet, leaving at least ½ inch between each dot. Let dry at room temperature for 24 hours before using.

FLAVORS

APPLE PIE

Part doughnut, part fried pie, these treats are all apple-y goodness. Tart pie apples, such as Granny Smiths, make the best filling.

MAKES 6 TO 12 DOUGHNUTS

1 cup cooking apples, cut into ¼-inch dice

2 tablespoons super-fine sugar

1 tablespoon freshly squeezed lemon juice

2 teaspoons arrow-root powder

1 teaspoon vanilla extract

¼ teaspoon ground allspice

¼ teaspoon ground cinnamon

1 batch Apple Cider (page 36) or Old-Fashioned Sour Cream (page 32) dough

1 tablespoon milk of choice or water, at room temperature

1 batch Cinnamon Spice (page 66) or Caramel (page 69) glaze

• In a medium heavy-bottomed pot over medium heat, combine the apples, sugar, and lemon juice and heat until the sugar is melted. Stir in the arrowroot, vanilla, allspice, and cinnamon. Simmer until the filling thickens, about 2 minutes. Remove from the heat and set aside.

• Prepare the chosen dough as directed, but roll it out to just a bit less than ½ inch thick. With a doughnut or cookie cutter, cut out 3-inch rounds. Roll out half of the rounds to about 3¼ inches.

• To assemble, lightly brush each wider dough round with the milk and place a tablespoon of the apple filling in the center. Spread it out evenly, leaving a ¼-inch margin around the edge. Top the filling with a smaller dough round and lightly pinch the top and bottom rounds together to seal. Then recut the doughnut with the same cutter, sealing the edges.

• Fry as directed and allow the dough-nuts to cool slightly before glazing.

APPLE-CHEDDAR FRITTERS

Whether or not it's a good thing to have a slice of sharp cheddar with your apple pie may be an age-old debate, but a subtle bite of cheddar in your apple fritters is sure to end any such quarrels.

MAKES 12 FRITTERS

1 batch raised dough of choice

1½ cups shredded sharp cheddar cheese, divided

1½ cups peeled and diced apple (about 2 medium apples)

2 tablespoons freshly squeezed lemon juice

2 tablespoons unsalted butter or coconut oil

½ cup brown sugar

1 tablespoon all-purpose flour

1 teaspoon ground cinnamon

½ teaspoon sea salt

1 batch glaze of choice (optional)

Flaky sea salt for garnish (optional)

• Prepare the chosen dough as directed, but reduce the butter specified by half and stir in 1 cup of the cheese along with it. Proceed with the dough through the initial chilled rise stage.

• While the dough rises, in a small bowl, put the apples and lemon juice, and stir to coat.

• In a medium skillet over medium-low heat, melt the butter. Stir in the apples, sugar, flour, cinnamon, and salt. Cook until the apples soften and the liquid becomes a syrup, about 15 minutes. Transfer the apple mixture to a bowl, cover with plastic wrap, and refrigerate until the dough has risen.

• Line a baking sheet with a lightly floured non-terry cloth dish towel.

• When the dough is ready, roll it out on a lightly floured surface to create a rectangle about ½ inch thick. Position the rectangle so a long end is closest to you. Spread a little more than half of the apple mixture over the bottom half of the dough, leaving about a 1-inch border, and then sprinkle about ¼ cup of the remaining cheese over the apples. Fold the top half of the dough over the apples to meet the bottom edge. Pinch the edges to seal.

• Rotate the dough 90 degrees, and sprinkle the remaining apple mixture and ¼ cup cheese over the bottom half. Fold the top half over the apples to meet the bottom edge, and pinch the edges to seal.

• Roll out the apple-filled dough to create a rectangle about ½ inch thick, then cut the dough into 12 (2½-inch) square fritters. Pull the corners of each fritter up and toward the center and pinch to seal. Place the fritters on the lined baking sheet, leaving at least 1 inch between.

• Cover with a towel or plastic wrap, and let the fritters proof for 5 to 20 minutes in a warm spot, then fry or bake as directed for the chosen dough. If frying, keep the oil temperature at 350 degrees F and fry until the fritters are a deep caramel color, about 3 minutes on each side.

• Glaze the cooled fritters and sprinkle with a tiny bit of sea salt.

NOTE: Try a splash of apple cider vinegar in the glaze for added tang.

PINEAPPLE FRITTERS

These fritters are like magic. Just a quick dip of batter puffs up to create a doughnut around the pineapple ring, trapping in the juicy goodness.

MAKES 6 FRITTERS

½ batch cake dough of choice

¼ cup water or milk of choice, at room temperature

Vegetable oil for frying

6 (½-inch-thick) pineapple rings

Confectioners' sugar for dusting

• Prepare the chosen dough as directed, adding the ¼ cup water so the mixture resembles a thick pancake batter.

• While the batter is resting, in a heavy-bottomed pot, heat at least 2 inches of oil until a deep-fat thermometer registers 360 degrees F.

• Dip each pineapple ring in the batter to coat.

• Fry for about 2 minutes on each side, or until the batter has puffed and become a rich caramel color.

• Remove with a slotted spoon. Drain on a wire rack set over a paper towel, and serve while still a little warm, dusted with sugar.

BANANA BREAD

Banana keeps these doughnuts tender, so they keep well for a day or two, but I can't resist them when they are still warm with a crisp crust.

MAKES 8 TO 12 DOUGHNUTS OR 25 TO 35 DROP DOUGHNUTS

1 batch cake dough of choice

1 banana, mashed

¼ cup pecans, chopped (optional)

Pinch of ground cardamom (optional)

1 batch Maple glaze (page 63)

• Prepare the chosen dough as directed, reducing the milk specified by a third (for example, ½ cup milk would become ⅓ cup). Mix in the banana, pecans, and cardamom after mixing the wet ingredients, and mix on low speed until just combined; be sure not to overmix or the doughnuts may end up rubbery.

• Pipe and fry the dough as directed and allow the doughnuts to cool slightly before glazing.

ORANGE-CRANBERRY CAKE

The smell of these doughnuts always transports me to the holidays. They are the perfect accompaniment to a warm fire and a cup of tea.

MAKES 8 TO 12 TRADITIONAL DOUGHNUTS OR 25 TO 35 DROP DOUGHNUTS

1 batch cake dough of choice

1 teaspoon ground cinnamon

¼ cup pecans, finely chopped (optional)

2 tablespoons dried cranberries

1 tablespoon freshly grated orange zest

1 batch Citrus glaze (page 64)

- Prepare the chosen dough as directed, replacing the nutmeg specified with the cinnamon. After mixing the wet ingredients, mix in the pecans, cranberries, and orange zest on low speed.

- Pipe and fry the dough as directed and allow the doughnuts to cool slightly before glazing.

CARROT CAKE

My friend Shauna makes the best carrot cake around. Her secret? Reduce the carrot juice to a syrup for intense carroty sweetness. Top these with a whipped cream cheese frosting or use the Basic Sugar glaze (page 58).

MAKES 8 TO 12 TRADITIONAL DOUGHNUTS OR 25 TO 35 DROP DOUGHNUTS

2 cups carrot juice

1 batch cake dough of choice

½ tablespoon ground ginger

½ tablespoon ground cinnamon

½ teaspoon ground cloves

½ cup finely grated carrot (about 1 large carrot)

¼ cup walnuts, finely chopped

¼ cup golden raisins

Cream Cheese Frosting (page 118)

¼ cup chopped pecans or sweetened shredded or flaked coconut (optional)

• In a small saucepan over medium heat, bring the carrot juice to a boil. Reduce the heat to low and simmer slowly, stirring occasionally, until the juice has reduced to about ½ cup, 20 to 30 minutes. Remove from the heat and let cool.

• Prepare the chosen dough as directed, replacing the specified nutmeg with the ginger, cinnamon, and cloves, and the milk specified with the carrot syrup (you may not use all the syrup). After mixing the wet ingredients, fold in the grated carrot, walnuts, and raisins.

• Pipe and fry the dough as directed. Allow the doughnuts to cool slightly before frosting. Spread the cooled doughnuts with the frosting and garnish with the pecans.

SWEET CORN DROPS

These cornbread-like doughnuts are best made in late summer when you can cut the corn off the cob yourself. But you can substitute frozen corn out of season as well. I also like to serve these drops with honey butter.

MAKES 25 TO 30 DROP DOUGHNUTS

1 batch cake dough of choice

¼ cup (40 grams) fine or medium grind cornmeal

¼ cup honey

1 teaspoon freshly grated lemon zest

¼ cup sweet corn

1 batch Honey glaze (page 62) (optional)

• Prepare the chosen dough as directed, replacing ¼ cup of the all-purpose flour with the cornmeal, the sugar specified with the honey, and the nutmeg specified with the lemon zest. After mixing the wet ingredients, fold in the corn.

• For rustic drop-style doughnuts, heat the oil to 330 degrees F. Drop rounded spoonfuls of the batter into the oil and fry until light golden brown, about 1 minute on each side.

• Let cool slightly before glazing.

MARGARITA

You're not likely to find tequila, lime, and salt topping the doughnuts in your local bakery. Good thing you can make them yourself! Fleur de sel adds a distinctive flavor and texture; if you can't find it, use another good-quality, flaky sea salt. For an extra kick of lime, try filling these doughnuts with lime curd (using the Basic Fruit Curd recipe on page 100).

MAKES 8 TO 14 DOUGHNUTS

1 batch raised dough of choice

1 teaspoon freshly grated lime zest, plus more for garnish (optional)

½ cup (60 grams) confectioners' sugar

2 teaspoons freshly squeezed lime juice (about ½ lime)

1 teaspoon tequila

Fleur de sel for garnish (optional)

• Prepare the chosen dough as directed, replacing the vanilla specified with the lime zest, and fry or bake as directed.

• To make the glaze, sift the sugar into a wide bowl large enough to dip the doughnut rounds in. Stir in the lime juice and tequila until smooth. Dip each cooled doughnut into the glaze and set on a wire rack to dry. Sprinkle with fleur de sel and lime zest.

FRUIT CURD FILLED

Fruit curds are tangier than typical fruit preserves, and they make a much more luscious filling for doughnuts. Any leftover curd is amazing stirred into yogurt or spread onto toast.

MAKES 8 TO 12 DOUGHNUTS

1 batch raised dough of choice

1 batch Basic Fruit Curd (recipe follows)

1 batch Basic Sugar (page 58) or Citrus (page 64) glaze

• Prepare the chosen dough for filled doughnuts and fry or bake as directed.

• When the doughnuts have cooled, spoon the fruit curd into a pastry bag fitted with a Bismarck (#230) tip. Holding a doughnut in one hand, plunge the tip into the side of the doughnut, pushing it about ¾ inch deep. Gently squeeze the pastry bag to fill the doughnut, withdrawing the tip slowly as you squeeze; you will feel the doughnut expand slightly as you fill it. Repeat with the remaining doughnuts. Glaze the top of each doughnut and let set before serving.

CONTINUED . . .

Basic Fruit Curd

You may have had lemon or lime curd before . . . but did you know you can make fruit curd from all sorts of fruits to get a tangy, creamy filling? Prepare the fruit curd before the dough, and let it cool while you make the doughnuts. Have curd left over? It's an amazing toast topper.

MAKES ABOUT 1 CUP

½ cup (100 grams) granulated sugar

5 egg yolks, lightly beaten

1 batch Citrus, Berry, or Stone Fruit Curd Flavoring (recipes follow)

4 tablespoons unsalted butter

• In the top of a double boiler (or in a nonreactive saucepan), whisk the sugar and egg yolks. Stir in the curd flavoring and heat over simmering water (or low heat, if using a saucepan), stirring constantly, until the mixture thickens slightly and a thermometer registers 160 degrees F, 10 to 15 minutes.

• Remove from the heat and stir in the butter, 1 tablespoon at a time, incorporating each piece completely before adding the next. Allow the mixture to cool to room temperature, cover with plastic wrap, and refrigerate for up to 2 weeks.

CITRUS CURD FLAVORING

¼ cup freshly squeezed citrus juice
2 tablespoons freshly grated citrus zest

• In a small bowl, combine the citrus juice and zest.

BERRY CURD FLAVORING

2 pints fresh berries
1 tablespoon freshly grated lemon zest

• In a medium saucepan over medium heat, heat
the berries just until they start to soften, about
5 minutes, then push through a fine-mesh sieve,
discarding the solids. Combine ¼ cup of the berry
juice with the lemon zest, and reserve the rest of
the juice for another use.

STONE FRUIT CURD FLAVORING

2 cups sliced juicy stone fruit (such as apricots, plums,
   or peaches)
Freshly squeezed juice of 1 lemon

• In a medium saucepan over medium heat, heat
the fruit until the slices fall apart, about 15 minutes.
Transfer to a blender and blend until smooth. Combine ½ cup of the puree with the lemon juice, and
reserve the rest of the puree for another use.

RHUBARB FILLED

Filled before they are fried, these doughnuts are like doughnut-crusted hand pies. You could always toss in a few strawberries with the rhubarb, but rhubarb's tartness is delicious on its own. I love these with the berry glaze.

MAKES ABOUT 8 TO 10 FILLED DOUGHNUTS

1 batch raised dough
 of choice

3 stalks rhubarb

½ cup (100 grams)
 granulated sugar

1 tablespoon all-
 purpose flour

1 teaspoon ground
 cinnamon

½ teaspoon sea salt

2 teaspoons unsalted
 butter or coconut oil

1 batch Berry glaze
 (page 72)

• Prepare the chosen dough as directed through the initial chilled rise stage.

• While the dough is rising, prepare the filling. Trim any woody ends from the rhubarb and peel off any particularly tough skin. Thinly slice the stalks (you should have about 2 cups), and place in a medium pot over low heat. Add the sugar, flour, cinnamon, and salt and toss to coat. Add the butter and increase the heat to medium-low.

• Cook until the rhubarb softens, about 15 minutes. Transfer the rhubarb mixture to a bowl, cover with plastic wrap, and refrigerate until the dough has risen.

• When the dough is ready, roll it out on a lightly floured surface to a bit more than ¼ inch thick. Cut it into 3-inch squares.

• To assemble, top half of the squares with a heaping teaspoon of the rhubarb mixture. Top each with an unfilled square and pinch the edges with the tines of a fork to seal.

• Cover with a towel or plastic wrap, and let the doughnuts proof for 5 to 20 minutes in a warm spot, then fry or bake as directed for the chosen dough. Let cool slightly before glazing.

SOUR CHERRY FILLED

What's better than sour cherry pie? A cherry tart with a raised doughnut as the crust.

MAKES 8 TO 12 DOUGHNUTS

2 cups fresh or frozen pitted tart pie cherries

2 tablespoons granulated sugar

1 tablespoon freshly squeezed lemon juice

1 teaspoon cornstarch

1 batch raised dough of choice

1 batch Almond glaze (page 73)

• In a medium pot over medium-low heat, bring the cherries, sugar, lemon juice, and cornstarch to a simmer. Simmer until syrupy, about 5 minutes. Transfer the cherry filling to a bowl, cover with plastic wrap, and refrigerate until needed.

• Prepare the chosen dough for filled doughnuts and fry or bake as directed.

• When the doughnuts have cooled, use a sharp knife to cut out a small divot in the top center (not the side) of the doughnut. Don't cut all the way through the doughnut. Repeat with the remaining doughnuts, and then fill each divot with a spoonful of the cooled cherry filling.

• Drizzle the tops with the glaze.

BOSTON & BAVARIAN CREAM

Rich, eggy pastry cream is the key to a perfect Boston or Bavarian Cream doughnut; the only difference between the two is the glaze, so it's easy to make a half-and-half batch.

MAKES 8 TO 12 DOUGHNUTS

1 cup whole milk

1 vanilla bean, split lengthwise

Pinch of kosher salt

¼ cup (60 grams) superfine sugar

1 tablespoon cornstarch

1 egg

1 tablespoon unsalted butter

1 batch raised dough of choice

1 batch Chocolate glaze (page 61)

Confectioners' sugar for dusting

• Start by making the pastry cream. Set a fine-mesh sieve over a medium bowl and set aside.

• In a medium heavy-bottomed pot over medium heat, combine the milk, vanilla bean, and salt. Simmer, stirring constantly.

• In a small bowl, whisk the superfine sugar and cornstarch. Beat in the egg. Warm the egg mixture by slowly drizzling in one-third of the hot milk, whisking constantly. Add the warmed egg mixture to the pot with the remaining hot milk. Continue to whisk over medium heat for about 2 minutes or until the mixture thickens. Immediately remove the pastry cream from the heat and pour through the sieve. Let the mixture cool for about 5 minutes, stirring occasionally to prevent a skin from forming. Add the butter and stir until blended.

• Cover the pastry cream with plastic wrap pressed directly onto its surface to prevent a skin from forming or any condensation from dripping onto it. Refrigerate for at least 1 hour and up to 2 days. If the mixture separates, just whisk briskly until creamy.

• Prepare the chosen dough for filled doughnuts and fry or bake as directed.

• When the doughnuts have cooled, spoon the pastry cream in a pastry bag fitted with a Bismarck (#230) tip. Holding a doughnut in one hand, plunge the tip into the side of the doughnut, pushing it about ¾ inch deep. Gently squeeze the pastry bag to fill the doughnut, withdrawing the tip slowly as you squeeze; you will feel the doughnut expand slightly as you fill it. Repeat with the remaining doughnuts.

• For Boston Cream doughnuts, glaze the tops with the chocolate glaze and allow it to set before serving. For Bavarian Cream doughnuts, dust each doughnut with confectioners' sugar.

HUCKLEBERRY CHEESECAKE

Blue mountain huckleberries were in season when I was experimenting with cheesecake-filled doughnuts, so they were an easy choice among the many fruits that would be delicious with this creamy filling. If huckleberries aren't available, try cherries, raspberries, strawberries, blueberries, or one of the fruit curds from the recipe on page 100.

MAKES 8 TO 12 DOUGHNUTS

1 batch raised dough of choice

2 ounces cream cheese, at room temperature

2 tablespoons sweetened condensed milk

1 tablespoon plus 1 teaspoon freshly squeezed lemon juice, divided

1 tablespoon sour cream or plain yogurt, at room temperature

½ cup fresh huckleberries

1 tablespoon superfine sugar

1 tablespoon milk of choice or water, at room temperature

Graham Cracker Topping (recipe follows) (optional)

• Prepare the chosen dough as directed to the initial chilled rise stage.

• While the dough rises, prepare the filling. In a small bowl, beat the cream cheese using a hand mixer until fluffy, about 2 minutes. Stir in the condensed milk, 1 tablespoon of the lemon juice, and the sour cream. Beat until smooth. Refrigerate for at least 1 hour before filling the doughnuts.

• In a heavy-bottomed pot over medium heat, combine the huckleberries, sugar, and remaining 1 teaspoon lemon juice and stir until the huckleberries release some of their juices and the sugar has dissolved, about 5 minutes. Remove from the heat, and set aside to cool.

• When the dough has risen, roll it out on a lightly floured surface to a bit more than ¼ inch thick. With a doughnut or cookie cutter, cut out 3-inch rounds. Roll out half of the rounds to about 3¼ inches.

• To assemble, lightly brush each wider dough round with the milk and place a heaping teaspoon of the cream cheese filling in the center. Top it with a scant teaspoon of huckleberry filling. Top these with the smaller dough rounds and lightly pinch the edges to seal. Then recut the doughnut with the same cutter, sealing the edges.

- Cover with a towel or plastic wrap and let the doughnuts proof for 5 to 20 minutes in a warm spot, then fry as directed for the chosen dough. While the doughnuts are still warm, dip the tops in the graham cracker mixture.

Graham Cracker Topping

MAKES ABOUT ½ CUP

½ cup graham cracker crumbs

1 tablespoon super-fine sugar

2 tablespoons unsalted butter, melted

- In a small bowl, mix the graham cracker crumbs, sugar, and butter.

STRAWBERRY SHORTCAKE

The Donut Man shop in Glendora, California, may not look like much from outside. Inside, however, if the season is right, you'll find out why folks flock there: strawberry shortcake doughnuts piled high with farm-fresh fruit. This version is a little easier to assemble but just as tasty. At the height of summer, take another hint from Donut Man and substitute juicy slices of fresh peaches.

MAKES 8 TO 12 DOUGHNUTS

1 batch Ricotta (page 35) or cake dough of choice

1 cup heavy cream

2 tablespoons confectioners' sugar, sifted, plus more for dusting (optional)

1 teaspoon vanilla extract

1 pint fresh strawberries, sliced

• Prepare the chosen dough, pipe it into rings, and fry or bake as directed.

• While the doughnuts are cooling, in a medium bowl, whip the cream, sugar, and vanilla until soft peaks form.

• Top each doughnut with a dollop of whipped cream and 2 or 3 tablespoons of strawberries, or cut the doughnuts in half and sandwich the whipped cream and strawberries in the middle. Dust the tops lightly with sugar.

GERMAN CHOCOLATE

When I was a child my favorite cake was German chocolate. I couldn't resist running a finger (or five) through the bowl of rich, nutty frosting before the cake was sliced. But these doughnuts are so heavenly, you'll want to devote every bit of frosting to the intended destination.

MAKES 8 TO 12 DOUGHNUTS

1 batch Chocolate
  Cake dough
  (page 28)
½ cup evaporated
  milk
½ cup (120 grams)
  superfine sugar
1 egg yolk, beaten
  with 1 teaspoon
  water

¼ cup (½ stick)
  unsalted butter
½ cup chopped
  pecans
½ cup unsweetened
  flaked coconut
1 teaspoon vanilla
  extract

• Prepare the doughnuts as directed and let cool.

• In a heavy-bottomed pot over medium heat, combine the milk, sugar, egg yolk, and butter and stir until thick, about 12 minutes. Remove from the heat and stir in the pecans, coconut, and vanilla. Continue to stir until the frosting cools, then spread about 1 tablespoon on top of each doughnut.

PECAN PIE

My grandparents had a pecan ranch in their younger days, and pecan pie was a staple in their house. I think they would highly approve of this doughnut version of their recipe.

MAKES 8 TO 12 DOUGHNUTS

2 cups dark brown sugar

¾ cup (1½ sticks) unsalted butter or coconut oil

1½ cups corn syrup

1 teaspoon kosher salt

1 tablespoon vanilla extract

4 eggs

1 cup pecan halves

1 batch raised dough of choice

1 batch Bourbon (page 68) or Caramel (page 69) glaze

• In a medium pot over medium heat, combine the sugar, butter, syrup, and salt. Stir for 2 minutes and then remove from the heat. Whisk in the vanilla.

• In a medium bowl, whisk the eggs. Whisk in ½ cup of the sugar mixture at a time until completely incorporated. Return the mixture to the pot and cook for about 15 minutes, stirring occasionally, until it thickens. Remove from the heat and allow to cool for about 5 minutes. Then transfer the mixture to an airtight container and refrigerate until chilled, at least 1 hour.

• Meanwhile, preheat the oven to 350 degrees F. Spread the pecans on a rimmed baking sheet and toast for 5 minutes. Use a spoon to mix them around, pulling the inner nuts to the edges of the pan and vice versa. Toast for another 5 minutes, then set aside to cool.

• While the filling is cooling, prepare the chosen dough for filled doughnuts and fry or bake as directed.

• When the doughnuts have cooled, spoon the filling into a pastry bag fitted with a Bismarck (#230) tip. Holding a doughnut in one hand, plunge the tip into the side of the doughnut, pushing it about ¾ inch deep. Gently squeeze the pastry bag to fill the doughnut, withdrawing the tip slowly as you squeeze; you will feel the doughnut expand slightly as you fill it. Repeat with the remaining doughnuts.

• Glaze each doughnut, then top with the pecans.

PUMPKIN PIE

When fall comes, it seems like you can't turn around without bumping into some new pumpkin fad. Buck the trend and make these pumpkin-pie-filled doughnuts any time of the year.

MAKES 8 TO 12 DOUGHNUTS

1 cup (7 ounces) pumpkin puree

2 tablespoons cornstarch

¼ cup (50 grams) brown sugar

2 tablespoons granulated sugar

1 teaspoon ground cinnamon

½ teaspoon ground ginger

¼ teaspoon ground nutmeg

¼ teaspoon kosher salt

½ cup milk of choice

1 tablespoon unsalted butter or coconut oil, melted

1 batch raised dough of choice

1 batch Brown Butter (page 67) or Cinnamon Spice (page 66) glaze

• In a large pot over medium-low heat, stir together the pumpkin puree, cornstarch, sugars, cinnamon, ginger, nutmeg, and salt. Add the milk, a little at a time, and stir to incorporate. If you have an immersion blender, feel free to use it here. Then stir in the butter. Increase the heat to medium and cook until the mixture thickens, about 10 minutes, stirring frequently, especially the bottom and sides of the pot.

• Remove from the heat and let stand for 10 minutes. Transfer to a medium bowl, cover with plastic wrap, and refrigerate for at least 1 hour.

• While the filling is cooling, prepare the chosen dough for filled doughnuts and fry or bake as directed.

• When the doughnuts have cooled, spoon the filling into a pastry bag fitted with a Bismarck (#230) tip. Holding a doughnut in one hand, plunge the tip into the side of the doughnut, pushing it about ¾ inch deep. Gently squeeze the pastry bag to fill the doughnut, withdrawing the tip slowly as you squeeze; you will feel the doughnut expand slightly as you fill it. Repeat with the remaining doughnuts.

• Glaze each doughnut before serving.

RED VELVET

Red velvet cake makes a dramatic presentation, and these doughnuts—with their deep-red, subtly chocolate cake and whipped cream cheese frosting—are equally impressive.

MAKES 8 TO 12 TRADITIONAL DOUGHNUTS OR 25 TO 35 DROP DOUGHNUTS

1 batch cake dough of choice

¼ cup (27 grams) Dutch processed cocoa powder

¼ cup (60 grams) superfine sugar

2 teaspoons red food coloring

2 teaspoons white vinegar

Cream Cheese Frosting (recipe follows)

¼ cup chopped pecans or unsweetened shredded or flaked coconut for garnish (optional)

• Prepare the chosen dough as directed, but omit the nutmeg specified and stir in the cocoa powder and additional sugar with the dry ingredients. Add the food coloring and vinegar to the wet ingredients.

• Pipe and fry or bake the doughnuts as directed.

• Spread the cooled doughnuts with the frosting and garnish with pecans.

Cream Cheese Frosting

MAKES ABOUT 1½ CUPS FROSTING

4 ounces cream cheese, at room temperature

1 cup (120 grams) confectioners' sugar, sifted

¼ cup (½ stick) unsalted butter, at room temperature

½ teaspoon vanilla extract

• In the bowl of a stand mixer fitted with the paddle attachment, whip the cream cheese, sugar, butter, and vanilla on low speed until creamy. Increase the speed to high and mix until light and fluffy, about 5 minutes, scraping down the sides of the bowl as needed. Cover with plastic wrap and refrigerate for at least 1 hour before using.

VARIATION: Whisk in 1 tablespoon strained raspberry or other fruit jam, or even a little bit of red food coloring, along with the vanilla.

CHOCOLATE CHOCOLATE CHIP

Chocolate chip doughnuts are delicious . . . but chocolate chocolate chip doughnuts are a chocolate lover's dream come true.

MAKES 8 TO 12 DOUGHNUTS

1 batch Chocolate
Cake dough
(page 28)

⅓ cup chocolate chips

1 batch Basic Sugar
glaze (page 58)

• Prepare the dough as directed; after mixing the wet ingredients, mix in the chocolate chips by hand.

• Roll out, cut, and fry the doughnuts as directed and allow them to cool slightly before glazing.

CANDY-FILLED CHOCOLATE DROPS

I spied this fun trick in a Martha Stewart *Everyday Food* magazine—little bite-size doughnut holes stuffed with caramel candy. As the doughnuts cook, the candy melts into a perfect oozy center. Caramel is a great option, but I say try your favorite candies: Reese's Peanut Butter Cups, Hershey's Kisses, Snickers, you name it.

MAKES 15 TO 20 DOUGHNUTS

1 batch Chocolate Cake dough (page 28)

Your favorite meltable candy, cut into 15 to 20 (½-inch) pieces

1 batch Basic Sugar glaze (page 58) (optional)

Confectioners' sugar or Dutch processed cocoa powder for dusting (optional)

• Prepare the dough as directed, rolling it out to about ¼ inch thick. Cut out 1-by-2-inch rectangles. Place a candy chunk about ½ inch in from one edge and fold the other edge over the top to enclose the candy. Press the edges lightly to seal, then fry as directed.

• Glaze or dust the doughnuts with sugar or cocoa powder.

COCOA NIB

Cocoa nibs add a subtle nutty taste and unexpected crunch to simple cake doughnuts. They work equally well with plain cake or chocolate cake dough.

MAKES 8 TO 12 TRADITIONAL DOUGHNUTS OR 25 TO 35 DROP DOUGHNUTS

1 batch cake dough of choice

¼ cup cocoa nibs

1 batch Basic Sugar glaze (page 58)

• Prepare the chosen dough as directed; after mixing the wet ingredients, mix in the cocoa nibs on low speed.

• Fry or bake the doughnuts as directed, and allow them to cool slightly before glazing.

MOCHA

Coffee and doughnuts come together in this decadent morning or evening treat.

MAKES 8 TO 12 DOUGHNUTS

1 batch Chocolate
 Cake dough
 (page 28)

2 tablespoons brewed
 espresso, divided

1 batch Chocolate
 glaze (page 61)

• Prepare the dough as directed, replacing the vanilla specified with 1½ tablespoons of the espresso.

• Make the chocolate glaze as directed, replacing the vanilla specified with the remaining ½ tablespoon espresso.

• Roll out, cut, and fry the doughnuts as directed, and allow them to cool slightly before glazing.

HOT CHOCOLATE

Kick your chocolate doughnuts up a notch with a bit of spice. A little cinnamon and cayenne pepper transform the ordinary chocolate cake doughnut into something special. For an added kick, mix a pinch of cayenne pepper into the glaze.

MAKES 8 TO 12 DOUGHNUTS

1 batch Chocolate Cake dough (page 28)

1 teaspoon ground cinnamon

½ teaspoon cayenne pepper

1 batch Basic Sugar (page 58) or Chocolate (page 61) glaze

• Prepare the dough as directed, adding the cinnamon and cayenne to the dry ingredients.

• Roll out, cut, and fry the doughnuts as directed, and allow them to cool slightly before glazing.

GRASSHOPPER

The grasshopper pie borrowed its name from the minty-chocolaty cocktail made with equal parts crème de menthe, crème de cacao, and cream. The pie upped the chocolate factor with its chocolate wafer cookie crust, so it seems only proper that a doughnut of the same name should up the chocolate factor even more with a chocolate doughnut.

MAKES 8 TO 12 DOUGHNUTS

1 batch of Chocolate Raised (page 11) or Chocolate Cake dough (page 28)

⅓ cup (27 grams) unsweetened dark cocoa powder (optional)

1½ cups (180 grams) confectioners' sugar, sifted

Pinch of kosher salt

¼ cup (2 ounces) green crème de menthe

¼ cup (2 ounces) clear crème de cacao

2 teaspoons vanilla extract

2 chocolate wafer cookies, crushed

• Prepare the chosen dough as directed, but replace the cocoa powder specified with the unsweetened dark cocoa powder. Fry the doughnuts as directed. Allow to cool while preparing the topping.

• In a medium bowl, mix the sugar and salt. In a small bowl, mix the crème de menthe, crème de cacao, and vanilla until combined. Stir the crème mixture into the sugar, a little at a time, to make a smooth, pourable glaze.

• Dip the top of each doughnut in the glaze, gently shaking to remove any excess. For an allover glaze, flip and dip the other side as well. Allow the glaze to set, 5 to 10 minutes. Sprinkle with a bit of crushed cookie and serve immediately.

S'MORES

Like s'mores around the campfire, these treats need to be eaten immediately while the chocolate and marshmallow are still ooey-gooey. If you want a similar doughnut that you can take with you to a party, fill them with marshmallow crème, then glaze with chocolate. The glaze really is optional, for when you want an intensely sweet hit; these doughnut s'mores are plenty sweet without it.

MAKES 8 TO 12 DOUGHNUTS

3 to 4 tablespoons unsalted butter, melted, divided

10 graham crackers, finely crushed

2 teaspoons superfine sugar

1 batch raised dough of choice

1 tablespoon milk of choice or water, at room temperature

12 (1-ounce) squares milk or dark chocolate

48 mini marshmallows

1 batch Basic Sugar (page 58) or Chocolate (page 61) glaze (optional)

• In a shallow bowl, stir together 3 tablespoons of the melted butter, the graham crackers, and sugar. Cover with plastic wrap and set aside.

• Prepare the chosen dough as directed through the initial chilled rise stage. Roll out the dough to just a bit more than ¼ inch thick. With a doughnut or cookie cutter, cut out 3-inch rounds. Roll out half of the rounds to about 3¼ inches.

• To assemble, lightly brush each wider dough round with the milk and place a square of chocolate and 4 mini marshmallows in the center. Top with the smaller dough rounds and lightly pinch the edges to seal. Then recut the doughnuts with the same cutter, sealing the edges.

• Fry or bake the doughnuts as directed and let cool for 3 minutes. Glaze the doughnuts or brush them with the remaining 1 tablespoon melted butter, then dip into the graham cracker mixture. Serve immediately.

CHOCOLATE-PEANUT BUTTER

Get your chocolate in your peanut butter with this doughnut version of a Reese's Peanut Butter Cup.

MAKES 8 TO 12 DOUGHNUTS

1 batch Chocolate Raised dough (page 11)

1 cup creamy peanut butter

3 tablespoons unsalted butter, at room temperature

⅔ cup (80 grams) confectioners' sugar

1 batch Chocolate (page 61) or Basic Sugar (page 58) glaze

• Prepare the dough for filled doughnuts and fry as directed.

• In a medium bowl, whip the peanut butter and butter using a hand mixer on medium speed until creamy. Sift in the sugar and beat on medium speed until light and fluffy, about 2 minutes. Spoon the peanut butter filling into a pastry bag fitted with a Bismarck

(#230) tip. Holding a doughnut in one hand, plunge the tip into the side of the doughnut, pushing it about ¾ inch deep. Gently squeeze the pastry bag to fill the doughnut, withdrawing the tip slowly as you squeeze; you will feel the doughnut expand slightly as you fill it. Repeat with the remaining doughnuts.

• Glaze the top of each doughnut and let set before serving.

CHOCOLATE-HAZELNUT FILLED

Chocolate-hazelnut spreads like Nutella or Loacker make an addictively delicious filling for raised doughnuts. Adding a little whipped cream lightens the spread a bit, making it a little less rich and a little easier to pipe into the doughnuts.

MAKES 8 TO 12 DOUGHNUTS

1 batch raised dough of choice

1 cup chocolate-hazelnut spread

½ cup heavy cream

1 batch Chocolate (page 61) or Basic Sugar (page 58) glaze

• Prepare the chosen dough for filled doughnuts and fry as directed.

• In a medium bowl, whip the chocolate-hazelnut spread and cream using a hand mixer on medium speed until smooth and fluffy. Spoon the filling into a pastry bag fitted with a Bismarck (#230) tip. Holding a doughnut in one hand, plunge the tip into the side of the doughnut, pushing it about ¾ inch deep. Gently squeeze the pastry bag to fill the doughnut, withdrawing the tip slowly as you squeeze; you will feel the doughnut expand slightly as you fill it. Repeat with the remaining doughnuts.

• Glaze the top of each doughnut and let set before serving.

CHOCOLATE CREAM FILLED

These chocolate cream–filled doughnuts are inspired by my childhood favorites from Dunkin' Donuts, in which the chocolate filling is more whipped cream than ganache. If you like your chocolate filling a bit richer, up the cocoa powder to 3 tablespoons.

MAKES 8 TO 12 DOUGHNUTS

1 batch raised dough of choice

1 cup heavy cream

1½ tablespoons Dutch processed cocoa powder

1 tablespoon super-fine sugar

½ teaspoon vanilla extract

Confectioners' sugar for rolling

• Prepare the chosen dough for filled doughnuts and fry as directed.

• In a large bowl, combine the cream, cocoa powder, sugar, and vanilla. Cover with plastic wrap and refrigerate for 15 minutes. Using a hand mixer on low speed or a whisk, whip the mixture to soft peaks.

• Spoon the filling into a pastry bag fitted with a ¼-inch star tip. Holding a doughnut in one hand, plunge the tip into the side of the doughnut, pushing it about ¾ inch deep. Gently squeeze the pastry bag to fill the doughnut, withdrawing the tip slowly as you squeeze; you will feel the doughnut expand slightly as you fill it. Repeat with the remaining doughnuts.

• Roll the cooled doughnuts in sugar and serve.

CHOCOLATE COCONUT MACAROON DOUGHNUT HOLES

These little coconut treats are quite rich, so I like to make bite-size holes rather than full rings. Stored in an airtight container, they are just as good the next day.

MAKES 15 TO 20 DOUGHNUT HOLES

1 batch Chocolate
   Cake dough
   (page 28)
9 tablespoons pas-
   teurized egg white
Pinch of cream of
   tartar

6 tablespoons super-
   fine sugar
1½ cups unsweetened
   shredded coconut,
   divided

• Prepare the dough as directed, cutting out 1-inch rounds. Fry as directed and allow the doughnut holes to cool slightly.

• Preheat the oven to 400 degrees F.

• In a stand mixer, beat the egg white and cream of tartar on medium speed for about 8 minutes, or until stiff. Gradually beat in the sugar until the meringue becomes smooth and glossy. Fold in ½ cup of the coconut.

• Put the remaining coconut in a shallow bowl and line a baking sheet with parchment paper. Dip most of each doughnut hole in the meringue, roll in the coconut to coat the meringue, and arrange on the baking sheet. Bake until the tops just start to brown, about 5 minutes. Cool on a wire rack before serving.

BRANDIED EGGNOG

Make the holiday season just a little more so with these festive dough-nuts. Sprinkling the tops with nutmeg not only adds a spicy zing but also gives them a tantalizing eggnog appearance.

MAKES 8 TO 12 TRADITIONAL DOUGHNUTS OR 25 TO 35 DROP DOUGHNUTS

1 batch cake dough of choice

¼ to ⅔ cup eggnog, at room temperature

2 to 3 tablespoons brandy, divided

1 batch Brown Butter glaze (page 67)

Freshly grated nutmeg for dusting (optional)

• Prepare the chosen dough as directed, reducing the sugar specified to 3 table-spoons and replacing the milk with the eggnog and the vanilla with 1 tablespoon of the brandy. Fry or bake as directed.

• Prepare the glaze as directed, replac-ing the milk specified with the remaining 1 to 2 tablespoons brandy.

• After the doughnuts have cooled slightly, glaze them and dust the tops with nutmeg before serving.

CRÈME BRÛLÉE

Fluffy pastry, creamy goodness, and a perfect caramel crackle: these doughnuts bring a new level of sophistication to a favorite treat.

MAKES 8 TO 12 DOUGHNUTS

½ cup whole milk

½ cup heavy cream

½ vanilla bean, split lengthwise

¾ cup (180 grams) superfine sugar, divided

2 egg yolks, at room temperature

1 batch raised dough of choice

• In a medium saucepan set over medium heat, bring the milk, cream, and vanilla bean to a simmer. Meanwhile, whisk ¼ cup of the sugar and the egg yolks in a large bowl until the mixture is a pale yellow, about 2 minutes. When the milk mixture is simmering, slowly pour it over the egg mixture, whisking constantly to prevent the eggs from curdling. Return the mixture to the saucepan and continue cooking until it thickens, 2 to 3 minutes. Remove from the heat and continue whisking until smooth. Pour the custard into a medium bowl and cover with plastic wrap, pressing it directly onto the surface of the custard to prevent a skin from forming. Refrigerate for at least 2 hours.

• Prepare the chosen dough for filled doughnuts and fry or bake as directed.

• Spoon the custard into a pastry bag fitted with a Bismarck (#230) tip. Holding a doughnut in one hand, plunge the tip into the side of the doughnut, pushing it about ¾ inch deep. Gently squeeze the pastry bag to fill the doughnut, withdrawing the tip slowly as you squeeze; you will feel the doughnut expand slightly as you fill it. Repeat with the remaining doughnuts.

• Dip the doughnut tops in the remaining ½ cup sugar to thickly coat, then place them sugar side up on a baking sheet. Sprinkle a little more sugar on top if needed. Use a kitchen torch to slowly caramelize the sugar until golden. (Alternatively, preheat the broiler to high and broil the doughnuts until the sugar is golden, 1 to 2 minutes.) Let cool so the sugar hardens.

PB&J

These PB&J doughnuts are seriously and deliciously messy. Eat them almost immediately or the doughnut will get soggy.

MAKES 8 TO 12 DOUGHNUTS

1 batch raised dough of choice

½ cup creamy peanut butter

2 tablespoons confectioners' sugar

2 tablespoons heavy cream

¼ cup raspberry jam

1 batch Honey glaze (page 62)

• Prepare the chosen dough for filled doughnuts and fry or bake as directed.

• In a medium bowl, beat the peanut butter, sugar, and cream until smooth and light. Cover with plastic wrap and refrigerate for about 15 minutes.

• Spoon the peanut butter cream into a pastry bag fitted with a Bismarck (#230) tip. Holding a doughnut in one hand, plunge the tip into the side of the doughnut, pushing it about ¾ inch deep. Gently squeeze the pastry bag to fill the doughnut, withdrawing the tip slowly as you squeeze; you will feel the doughnut expand slightly as you fill it. Repeat with the remaining doughnuts.

• Spoon the jam into another pastry bag fitted with the same size Bismarck tip. Fill the doughnuts through the same hole, angling the tip up slightly, being careful not to puncture the surface of the doughnut.

• Glaze the top of each doughnut and allow to set before serving.

PEANUT BUTTER POWDER FLUFFERNUTTER

Peanut butter powder recently found its way onto supermarket shelves (although if you can't find it in your local grocery store, you can order it online), and I can think of no better use of it than these outrageously sticky fluffernutter doughnuts.

MAKES 8 TO 12 DOUGHNUTS

1 batch raised dough of choice

1 cup marshmallow crème

¼ cup creamy peanut butter

1 tablespoon cream or milk of choice, at room temperature

Unsalted butter for greasing

2 cups peanut butter powder

• Prepare the chosen dough for filled doughnuts and fry or bake as directed.

• While the doughnuts are cooling, whisk the marshmallow crème, peanut butter, and cream. Grease the inside of a pastry bag with butter (this will keep the marshmallow mixture from sticking) and fit it with a ½-inch star tip. Fill with the marshmallow mixture.

• Put the peanut butter powder in a bag, and shake each cooled doughnut to coat. Place the coated doughnut on its edge in a bread or cake tin, so that it can be easily filled from the top.

• Use a skewer or chopstick to create a hole in the top of each doughnut, then gently squeeze in about 2 tablespoons of the marshmallow mixture. Repeat with the remaining doughnuts.

COCONUT CREAM FILLED

Coconut cream makes a great filling for just about any raised dough, but goes particularly well with Malasadas (page 18) to make the perfect tropical doughnut.

MAKES 8 TO 12 DOUGHNUTS

1 (14-ounce) can coconut milk, or 1¾ cups Homemade Coconut Milk (page 75)

⅓ cup (80 grams) superfine sugar

¼ cup plain almond milk

2 tablespoons cornstarch

1 tablespoon chia seeds (optional)

1 batch raised dough of choice

1 batch Coconut glaze (page 74)

1 cup sweetened shredded coconut

• In a medium pot over medium-low heat, stir the coconut milk and sugar with a wooden spoon or until the sugar has dissolved and the mixture has thickened slightly, about 5 minutes.

• In a small bowl, whisk the almond milk and cornstarch. Pour, whisking constantly, into the hot coconut milk mixture. Simmer for about 5 minutes, or until thickened. Stir in the chia seeds, transfer to a medium bowl, and cover with plastic wrap. Refrigerate until needed.

• Prepare the chosen dough for filled doughnuts and fry or bake as directed.

• When the doughnuts have cooled, spoon the coconut filling into a pastry bag fitted with a Bismarck (#230) tip. Holding a doughnut in one hand, plunge the tip into the side of the doughnut, pushing it about ¾ inch deep. Gently squeeze the pastry bag to fill the doughnut, withdrawing the tip slowly as you squeeze; you will feel the doughnut expand slightly as you fill it. Repeat with the remaining doughnuts.

• Glaze the top of each doughnut and sprinkle with the shredded coconut. Serve immediately.

NOTE: If you are making homemade coconut milk for the coconut milk glaze, prepare the milk first, then finish the glaze as the doughnuts are cooling. If you are using prepared coconut milk for the glaze, you can make the glaze as the doughnuts are cooling.

HONEY YOGURT FILLED

While you don't want to let these doughnuts sit for too long, I recommend at least a 15-minute resting period after filling, to let the yogurt mixture integrate with the doughnut crumb.

MAKES 8 TO 12 DOUGHNUTS

2 cups plain full-fat
  Greek yogurt

¼ cup honey

1 batch raised dough
  of choice

1 batch Honey glaze
  (page 62)

• In a medium bowl, mix the yogurt and honey. Cover with plastic wrap and refrigerate until needed.

• Prepare the chosen dough for filled doughnuts and fry or bake as directed.

• When the doughnuts have cooled, spoon the yogurt filling into a pastry bag fitted with a Bismarck (#230) tip. Holding a doughnut in one hand, plunge the tip into the side of the doughnut, pushing it about ¾ inch deep. Gently squeeze the pastry bag to fill the doughnut, withdrawing the tip slowly as you squeeze; you will feel the doughnut expand slightly as you fill it. Repeat with the remaining doughnuts.

• Glaze the top of each doughnut and let sit for 15 minutes before serving.

DULCE DE LECHE

When it comes to pastry, dulce de leche is often paired with churros. But raised doughnuts stuffed with fluffy dulce de leche whipped cream are worthy of a new tradition. Try a sprinkle of flaky sea salt to balance out the rich caramel flavors.

MAKES 8 TO 12 DOUGHNUTS

1 batch raised dough of choice

1 cup heavy cream

1 cup Homemade Dulce de Leche (recipe follows) or store-bought, divided

Flaky sea salt for garnish

- Prepare the chosen dough for filled doughnuts and fry or bake as directed.

- While the doughnuts are cooling, in a medium bowl, whip the cream to stiff peaks using a hand mixer. Fold in ½ cup of the dulce de leche. Refrigerate, covered with plastic wrap, until needed.

- When the doughnuts have cooled, spoon the whipped cream into a pastry bag fitted with a Bismarck (#230) tip. Holding a doughnut in one hand, plunge the tip into the side of the doughnut, pushing it about ¾ inch deep. Gently squeeze the pastry bag to fill the doughnut, withdrawing the tip slowly as you squeeze; you will feel the doughnut expand slightly as you fill it. Repeat with the remaining doughnuts.

- Drizzle the filled doughnuts with the remaining ½ cup dulce de leche and garnish with sea salt.

CONTINUED . . .

Homemade Dulce de Leche

There are about as many different recipes for dulce de leche as there are grains of sand on the beach. I'm scared of exploding cans of caramel, so I avoid the ones that heat sweetened condensed milk still in the can. For this recipe, I'm sticking with the simplest, although not the quickest, version that is just the basics. You'll need about three hours for the milk to transform into the luscious jam for these doughnuts. Don't have the time? You can skip the homemade dulce de leche and use store-bought if you'd like.

MAKES ABOUT 1 CUP

1 quart whole milk

1½ cups granulated sugar

¼ teaspoon kosher salt

½ teaspoon baking soda

1 teaspoon vanilla extract

• In a 4-quart pot over medium heat, combine the milk, sugar, and salt. Simmer, stirring occasionally, until the sugar dissolves. Add the baking soda and stir to combine. Reduce the heat to low and continue to simmer, stirring occasionally, for about 3 hours, or until the mixture is a rich dark-golden color and has reduced to about 1 cup. Remove from the heat and stir in the vanilla.

• Transfer the dulce de leche to a jar with a lid and refrigerate for up to 1 month.

SESAME

These sesame-encrusted doughnut holes are a play on the Chinese fried sesame dumplings *jian dui*. Those little balls are hollow and typically filled with sweet bean paste or custard. These treats use traditional raised dough for an unexpected East-meets-West bite.

MAKES 20 TO 30 DOUGHNUT HOLES

1 batch raised dough of choice

2 cups white sesame seeds

2 cups water

1 batch Basic Sugar glaze (page 58)

1 teaspoon toasted sesame oil

• Prepare the chosen dough as directed through the initial chilled rise stage.

• In a medium bowl, put the sesame seeds, and in another put the water.

• Line a baking sheet with a lightly floured non-terry cloth dish towel and set aside.

• On a lightly floured surface, roll out the dough to ½ inch thick. With a doughnut or cookie cutter, cut out 1-inch circles, or with a knife cut out 1-inch squares.

• Dip each of the dough pieces into the water and then into the sesame seeds, rolling them around to coat. Place on the prepared baking sheet, leaving at least ½ inch between each hole.

• Cover with plastic wrap, and let them rise in a warm spot for about 10 minutes, and then fry or bake as directed.

• While the doughnuts are cooling, prepare the glaze without the vanilla specified, instead adding the sesame oil with the milk. Dip each doughnut hole in the glaze and let the glaze firm slightly before serving.

GINGERBREAD

Want a little twist to your gingerbread? Make these with the chocolate cake dough. The spices go beautifully with chocolate.

MAKES 8 TO 12 TRADITIONAL DOUGHNUTS OR 25 TO 35 DROP DOUGHNUTS

1 teaspoon ground cinnamon

1 teaspoon ground ginger

Pinch of ground cloves

1 batch cake dough of choice

⅓ cup brown sugar

2 tablespoons molasses

1 batch Ginger glaze (page 71)

2 tablespoons crystallized ginger chips (optional)

• In a small bowl, mix the ginger, cinnamon, and cloves.

• Prepare the chosen dough as directed, replacing the nutmeg specified with the spice mixture and the superfine sugar with the brown sugar. Add the molasses along with the vanilla. Fry or bake the doughnuts as directed.

• After the doughnuts have cooled slightly, glaze them and sprinkle with the ginger chips.

PISTACHIO

To make coarsely ground pistachios, simply use a food processor and pulse shelled pistachios until they just start to give up some of their oils, about three to four minutes, scraping down the sides of the bowl as needed.

MAKES 8 TO 12 TRADITIONAL DOUGHNUTS OR 25 TO 35 DROP DOUGHNUTS

½ teaspoon ground cardamom

¼ teaspoon almond extract

⅓ cup pistachios, coarsely ground

⅔ cup pistachios, coarsely chopped, divided

1 batch cake dough of choice

1 batch Honey glaze (page 62)

Flaky sea salt for garnish

• Prepare the chosen dough as directed, replacing the nutmeg specified with the cardamom, reducing the vanilla extract to ½ teaspoon, and adding the almond extract to the wet ingredients. Mix in the ground pistachios and ⅓ cup of the chopped pistachios on medium speed. Fry or bake the doughnuts as directed.

• After the doughnuts have cooled slightly, glaze them and sprinkle with the remaining ⅓ cup pistachios. Garnish with sea salt and serve.

HERB & SPICE

Take simple cake doughnuts from ordinary to intriguing with just a hint of herbs and spices. Lavender pairs beautifully with vanilla, as long as you are careful and don't overdo it. Fennel seeds don't usually find their way into sweets, but an artful blending with orange brings out their nutty side. Browse your spice drawer and see what other combinations you can try.

MAKES 8 TO 12 TRADITIONAL DOUGHNUTS OR 25 TO 35 DROP DOUGHNUTS

1 batch Old-Fashioned Sour Cream (page 32) or cake dough of choice

Spice mixture of choice (recipes follow)

1 batch Basic Sugar glaze (page 58)

• Prepare the chosen dough as directed, omitting the nutmeg specified. After mixing the wet ingredients, fold in the chosen spice mixture. Fry or bake as directed, and allow the doughnuts to cool slightly before glazing.

Rosemary & Honey

1 tablespoon honey

1 teaspoon finely chopped fresh rosemary

• In a small bowl, combine the honey and rosemary.

Lavender & Vanilla

1 tablespoon vanilla extract

1 teaspoon finely chopped culinary lavender

• In a small bowl, combine the vanilla and lavender.

Fennel & Orange

1 tablespoon freshly grated orange zest

1 teaspoon fennel seeds, toasted and crushed

• In a small bowl, combine the orange zest and fennel seeds.

Poppy Seed & Lemon

2 tablespoons freshly grated lemon zest

1 tablespoon poppy seeds

• In a small bowl, combine the lemon zest and poppy seeds.

SWEET & SPICY

I love the pairing of habanero with tropical fruit, but if you aren't a fan of superhot, feel free to use jalapeño or a milder pepper.

MAKES 8 TO 12 TRADITIONAL DOUGHNUTS OR 25 TO 35 DROP DOUGHNUTS

4 tablespoons seeded and minced habanero or jalapeño, divided

1 medium mango, cubed

½ cup rice wine vinegar

¾ cup (180 grams) superfine sugar

1 tablespoon freshly squeezed lime juice

1 tablespoon freshly grated lime zest

1 batch cake dough of choice

• In a small pot over medium-low heat, stir together 1 tablespoon of the habanero, the mango, sugar, vinegar, and lime juice and zest. Simmer for about 5 minutes, or until the mixture has become slightly syrupy. Transfer to a blender and blend until smooth. Cover with plastic wrap and refrigerate until needed.

• Prepare the chosen dough as directed, adding the remaining 3 tablespoons habanero at the same time as the sugar, and fry or bake as directed. Allow to cool and frost each doughnut with the cooled hot sauce.

ALMOND-SEA SALT CARAMEL SUGARED

I learned this trick for making caramel powder from Kamran Siddiqi's terrific blog, *Sophisticated Gourmet*. He uses it to make quick work of crème brûlée (which you could do as well for the Crème Brûlée doughnuts on page 144), but the powder on its own is terrific for dusting doughnuts, especially when a little sea salt and almonds are mixed in.

MAKES 8 TO 12 TRADITIONAL DOUGHNUTS OR 25 TO 35 DROP DOUGHNUTS

1½ cups (300 grams) granulated sugar

1 cup whole almonds, toasted

½ teaspoon kosher salt

1 batch dough of choice

• Preheat the oven to 400 degrees F.

• Line a small rimmed baking sheet with parchment paper and spread the sugar on it evenly.

• Bake the sugar until mostly melted and golden, about 15 minutes, watching carefully so that it does not burn and removing it if needed. Remove from the oven and push any unmelted sugar bits into the melted sugar to even it out. Allow the sugar to cool and harden completely for about 20 minutes.

• Break the caramel into pieces, and put it in a blender or food processor along with the almonds and salt. Pulse to create a fine powder and set aside.

• Prepare the chosen dough and fry or bake as directed. Allow to cool slightly. Put the caramel powder in a paper bag, add a doughnut, and shake to coat. Or place the caramel powder in a shallow dish and dip the top of each doughnut in it. Either way is delicious! Repeat with the remaining doughnuts.

CHAI

I still recall the sweet, spicy warmth of my first cup of chai. By infusing the milk with black tea, you create a true chai flavor in every bite of doughnut.

MAKES 8 TO 12 TRADITIONAL DOUGHNUTS OR 25 TO 35 DROP DOUGHNUTS

1 cup whole milk

2 tablespoons black tea leaves or 2 tea bags

½ teaspoon ground ginger

½ teaspoon ground cinnamon

½ teaspoon freshly ground cardamom, plus more for the glaze (optional)

½ teaspoon freshly grated nutmeg

¼ teaspoon freshly ground black pepper

1 batch cake dough of choice

1 batch Basic Sugar glaze (page 58)

• In a medium pot over medium heat, scald the milk (see page 21) and add the tea leaves. Steep for about 5 minutes, then strain.

• In a small bowl, mix the ginger, cinnamon, cardamom, nutmeg, and pepper.

• Prepare the chosen dough as directed, replacing the nutmeg specified with the spice mixture and the plain milk with an equal amount of the tea-infused milk. Reserve the remaining tea-infused milk for the glaze. Fry or bake the doughnuts as directed.

• Prepare the glaze as directed, replacing the plain milk with an equal amount of the tea-infused milk and adding a pinch of cardamom.

• After the doughnuts have cooled slightly, glaze them and serve.

DATE-WALNUT

Inspired by a dense, dark tea cake, these doughnuts combine the same sticky, sweet dates and nutty walnut crunch, but in a lighter pastry. Lightly toasting the walnuts until fragrant gets rid of any bitterness.

MAKES 8 TO 12 TRADITIONAL DOUGHNUTS OR 25 TO 35 DROP DOUGHNUTS

1 batch Apple Cider (page 36) or cake dough of choice

¼ cup Medjool dates, finely chopped

¼ cup lightly toasted walnuts, finely chopped

1 batch Maple glaze (page 63)

• Prepare the chosen dough as directed. After mixing the wet ingredients, fold in the dates and walnuts.

• Fry or bake the doughnuts as directed and allow to cool slightly before glazing.

RAINBOW CAKE

Embrace the mess with these fun treats! You may end up with colorful batter everywhere, but it's worth the smiles these doughnuts bring. Be sure to place the three-color coupler in the pastry bags and attach them all together with the tip and ring before filling the bags or you'll have even more of a mess.

MAKES 8 TO 12 TRADITIONAL DOUGHNUTS OR 25 TO 35 DROP DOUGHNUTS

1 batch cake dough of choice

⅛ teaspoon each of 3 different gel food colorings

1 batch glaze of choice

Sprinkles for garnish

• Prepare the chosen dough as directed, adding all of the milk, as you want the batter looser than usual. Instead of resting the batter, divide it into thirds. Put the first third in the mixer and add the food coloring of the lightest shade. Mix on low speed until well incorporated. Transfer the batter into one of three pastry bags. Set aside. If needed, wipe the mixing bowl and beater before repeating with the next-lightest color. Finish with darkest color.

• Attach the three bags together, pipe, and fry or bake the doughnuts as directed. After the doughnuts have cooled slightly, glaze them. Go crazy and top with sprinkles!

NOTE: Don't want to deal with the pastry bag mess? Put the colored batters side by side in a large bowl, and make marbled drop doughnuts by scooping across all three colors with a soup spoon and then frying.

CARAMEL CORN

I'm not sure which is more addictive, doughnuts or caramel corn. Putting them both together means I don't have to solve this delicious dilemma.

MAKES 8 TO 12 DOUGHNUTS

1 tablespoon coconut oil, plus more for greasing

⅓ cup popcorn kernels

⅓ cup peanuts (optional)

⅓ cup pecans (optional)

⅓ cup slivered almonds (optional)

⅓ cup unsweetened shredded coconut (optional)

1 cup (200 grams) granulated sugar

2 tablespoons water

1 tablespoon corn syrup or brown rice syrup

½ teaspoon kosher salt

1 teaspoon baking soda

Flaky sea salt (optional)

Red pepper flakes (optional)

1 batch dough of choice

1½ batches Caramel glaze (page 69)

• Preheat the oven to 350 degrees F.

• In a large heavy-bottomed pot, heat the coconut oil over medium heat until melted. Add the popcorn to the pot, cover, and shake the pot occasionally until the popping stops. Transfer to a very large bowl. The bowl should be only about half full so you have plenty of room to toss the popcorn.

• Spread the nuts and coconut on a rimmed baking sheet and toast until fragrant, about 5 minutes. Add them to the bowl.

• Line a baking sheet with aluminum foil and set aside. Grease a large spoon and set aside (greasing the spoon will help keep the caramel from sticking to it).

• In a large heavy-bottomed pot over medium-low heat, bring the sugar, water, corn syrup, and kosher salt to a boil, stirring constantly and brushing down any errant crystals that form on the side of the pot. Once the sugar is boiling, reduce the heat to low. Stir occasionally until the mixture reaches 310 degrees F on a candy thermometer. This may take up to 20 minutes, so be patient. Rotate the pot every 5 minutes to avoid hot spots, and carefully watch the temperature, as it may change quickly when approaching 300 degrees F. When the sugar reaches 310 degrees F, remove it from the heat and stir in the baking soda. The caramel mixture may foam up.

• Pour the caramel mixture over the popcorn and nuts, and use the greased spoon (not your hands, as the mixture will be very, very hot) to stir to coat. Dump the coated popcorn onto the prepared baking sheet. Sprinkle with the sea salt and red pepper flakes. Let the caramel cool and harden for at least 15 minutes.

• Prepare the chosen dough and fry or bake as directed. After the doughnuts have cooled, dip one into the glaze and then into the caramel corn, which should stick to the wet glaze. With your hands, fill any gaps in the caramel corn if needed. When all the doughnuts are topped, drizzle them with the remaining caramel glaze.

PUFFED RICE TREATS

Puffed rice treats by themselves are a perfectly crazy topping for your doughnuts, but feel free to add in chocolate chips, peanut butter candies, and nuts for an even more over-the-top treat.

MAKES 8 TO 12 DOUGHNUTS

1 batch dough of choice

2 cups marshmallows

2 tablespoons unsalted butter

¼ teaspoon kosher salt

2 cups puffed rice cereal

1½ batches Basic Sugar glaze (page 58)

2½ ounces dark or milk chocolate, coarsely chopped

Flaky sea salt for garnish

• Prepare the chosen dough and fry or bake as directed. Allow to cool while preparing the topping.

• In a medium pot over low heat, cook the marshmallows and butter until melted, 3 to 4 minutes. Stir in the kosher salt. Add the cereal and stir to coat.

• Lay a piece of wax paper on a clean surface.

• Dip the top of a doughnut in the glaze, and then spoon on about 2 tablespoons of the cereal mixture. Gently push the doughnut, topping side down, onto the wax paper to even out the top. Repeat with the remaining doughnuts.

• In a double boiler over medium heat, or in a bowl over a bowl of hot water, melt the chocolate. Use a spoon to drizzle the melted chocolate over the topping, and sprinkle with a bit of sea salt.

MAPLE-BACON BARS

The salty sweetness of these bars are like the perfect pancake and bacon breakfast. If you want even more bacon flavor, try replacing the shortening in the dough with bacon grease. Don't eat bacon? Try these bars with a sprinkle of flaky smoked sea salt instead.

MAKES 8 TO 12 DOUGHNUTS

1 batch raised dough
  of choice

6 strips bacon

1 batch Maple glaze
  (page 63)

• Prepare the chosen dough as directed, cutting into 2-by-4-inch rectangles instead of rings. Fry or bake as directed and let cool slightly.

• In a large skillet over medium-high heat, fry the bacon until crisp, about 2 minutes on each side. Drain on paper towels, cool, and cut each strip in half crosswise.

• Dip each bar into the glaze, then top with a piece of bacon. Let the glaze set before serving.

CHICKEN & DOUGHNUTS

Move over, chicken and waffles. Chicken and doughnuts with a creamy maple glaze are the ultimate brunch indulgence.

MAKES 8 TO 12 DOUGHNUTS

6 boneless chicken thighs (about 2 pounds)

1 cup buttermilk

2 teaspoons kosher salt

1 batch raised dough of choice

2 cups (240 grams) all-purpose flour

½ teaspoon paprika

1 batch Maple glaze (page 63)

• Cut each chicken thigh in half and put in a gallon-size ziplock bag. Pour in the buttermilk and salt. Seal the bag and gently shake to coat the chicken pieces with the buttermilk. Refrigerate until ready to cook.

• Prepare the chosen dough for rings and fry as directed. Keep the oil at 360 degrees F.

• While the doughnuts are cooling, whisk together the flour and paprika in a shallow dish. Dip a chicken piece into the flour and turn to coat. Return the chicken to the buttermilk, then to the flour again, for a double coating. Repeat with another 2 to 3 pieces of chicken.

• Fry the chicken in the same oil you fried the doughnuts in, being careful not to overcrowd the pot, for 5 to 7 minutes total, flipping at least once. Remove the chicken from the oil, and drain on a wire rack set over paper towels. Use an instant-read thermometer to ensure the internal temperature of the chicken is 165 degrees F. Repeat the coating and frying process with the remaining chicken pieces.

• Top each doughnut with a piece of chicken and drizzle with the maple glaze. Serve immediately while the chicken is still warm.

DOUGHNUT-MAKING RESOURCES & SUPPLIES

You can find specialty doughnut-making equipment at most kitchen supply stores. Here are a few additional suggestions to help you along:

Bob's Red Mill Natural Foods
www.bobsredmill.com
Specialty flours (including gluten-free)

Crate and Barrel
www.crateandbarrel.com
Thermometers, pastry cloth

King Arthur Flour
www.kingarthurflour.com
Specialty flours (including gluten-free); doughnut cutters, pans, makers, mixes; glazing sugar; pastry cloth

Sur La Table
www.surlatable.com
Doughnut cutters, pastry bags, astry cloths, pastry bag tips, thermometers, deep fryers

Target
www.target.com
Doughnut pans and droppers, deep fryers

ThermoWorks
www.thermoworks.com
Thermapen thermometers

Williams Sonoma
www.williams-sonoma.com
Pastry bags with filling tips, deep fryers, thermometers, pastry cloth, doughnut cutters

ACKNOWLEDGMENTS

An enormous thank-you to the wonderful team at Sasquatch Books. From your initial excitement about this project and faith in me throughout the book's development, you've been a pillar of support in just the right way.

I was inspired and educated by a wide variety of sources, but there are a couple of noteworthy ones that taught me how to make doughnuts in the first place. The first successful cake doughnuts I made were from a recipe on JoePastry.com—a site that features recipes and tips that really work. I have not found a better source for learning pastry techniques than Bo Friberg's *The Professional Pastry Chef*, and without it I might never have arrived at my raised dough recipes.

A special thank-you to Shauna and Danny Ahern for their wonderful insights into gluten-free baking. Yes, you can make doughnuts gluten-free!

A huge thanks to my recipe testers: Bria Mertens, Caitlin Pierce, Carolyn Cope, Carolyn Pickton, Clair Sutton, Deeba Rajpal, Aparna Balasubramanian, Elizabeth Nyland, Helen McSweeney, Jamie Schler, Jennifer Eggleston, Jill Lightner, Linda Nguyen, Susan Roxborough, Anda, Lucy Vaserfirer, Andrew Vaserfirer, Maggie McConnell, Melinda Knapp, Cindy Ensley, M. Lynn Yu, Sheena Starky, Jess Thomson, Tom Bauer, Danielle Tsi, Tara Barker, and Tara O'Brady. Your great comments and questions made both the book and the doughnuts better!

I owe both Matt Wright and David Silver a debt and some doughnuts for graciously lending me their cameras after mine died midway through the photo shoot.

Finally, I never would have attempted to write this book without the encouragement, gentle nudging, and honest feedback from my wonderful husband, Cameron. You said I should do it and you were right.

INDEX

NOTE: Page numbers in *italic* refer to photographs.

ABOUT THE AUTHOR

Lara Ferroni is a tech geek turned food geek who spends her days exploring food and cocktail culture. You might spy her learning to make kimchi in the back room of a local church, foraging for wild berries, or snapping photos in some of the finest kitchens and bars. A writer and photographer, she is the author of five cookbooks, including *An Avocado a Day*, *Real Snacks*, and *Put an Egg on It*. You can find more of her tasty photos and recipes on her website, LaraFerroni.com.

Text and photography copyright
© 2010, 2018 by Lara Ferroni

All rights reserved. No portion of this
book may be reproduced or utilized in any
form, or by any electronic, mechanical,
or other means, without the prior written
permission of the publisher.

Printed in China

SASQUATCH BOOKS with colophon
is a registered trademark of
Penguin Random House LLC

Originally published in hardcover in the
United States by Sasquatch Books in 2018.

27 26 25 24 23   9 8 7 6 5 4 3 2 1

Editor: Susan Roxborough
Production editor: Bridget Sweet
Photographs: Lara Ferroni
Design: Bryce de Flamand
Copyeditor: Kirsten Colton

Library of Congress Cataloging-in-
Publication Data is available.

ISBN: 978-1-63217-524-3

Sasquatch Books
1325 Fourth Avenue, Suite 1025
Seattle, WA 98101

SasquatchBooks.com

MIX
Paper | Supporting
responsible forestry
FSC® C008047